The Nature of Human Society

NEW NATIONS

THE NATURE OF HUMAN SOCIETY SERIES
Editors: Julian Pitt-Rivers and Ernest Gellner

NEW
NATIONS

Lucy Mair

THE UNIVERSITY OF CHICAGO PRESS

THE UNIVERSITY OF CHICAGO PRESS, CHICAGO 60637
Weidenfeld and Nicolson, London W.1, England

International Standard Book Number: 0-226-50275-9
Library of Congress Catalog Card Number: 63-20917

CONTENTS

PREFACE

ONE OF the crucial events of the mid-twentieth century is the emergence to political independence of the majority of the peoples whom the nineteenth century brought under colonial rule. The political expansion of Europe was made possible by the superiority of Europe's technical knowledge, and the same technical knowledge enabled Europeans to develop the material resources of tropical territories and bring them into the world economic system. The new rulers of these territories are committed to go on with this process, and even hope to accelerate it.

The process is essentially that of increasing the scale of economic operations. This is not possible unless the scale of political and social relationships is also increased. The theme of this book is the effect of this increase in scale in different areas of the life of the people experiencing it.

There is a great mass of literature devoted to changes in the customs of non-European peoples under the influence of contact with the dominant European nations; of course this contact began before Europeans had gained the immense technical superiority that power-driven machinery gave them, but before the industrial revolution they had less need and less ability to reorganise other people's lives. Most of the literature starts from the assumption that when people are confronted with different customs from those they have been brought up to, they adopt some of them, reject others and 're-work' or 'reinterpret' those that they adopt. This approach is capable of considerable refinement. But implied in it there is always the assumption that we are dealing with a sort of jigsaw puzzle of items of behaviour, the property of a personified population who decide whether or not they will replace one of the existing pieces by one from another picture. This is the approach through the study of *culture*.

My approach is made through the study of *society*. This alternative approach leads to quite a different way of looking at what is happening. If one sees society as consisting of people linked by mutual rights and obligations, exercising choice where choice is open to them, pursuing their own advantage as they understand it, disregarding their obligations when they think they can get away with it, one can see the entry into the large-scale society as an expansion of the existing field of choice by the creation of new situations offering new opportunities. But the choice is not essentially between different customs or 'ways of life'; it is between the authority of the village headman and that of the employer, between the community of kin or age-mates and that of a church or a trade union, between dependence on the family herds and on the market for cattle. Of course the entry into new relationships is likely to involve changes in 'ways' which proclaim a new status: a clerk in an office is expected to, and likes to, wear a neat suit, though there is no reason why he could not do the job equally well dressed in barkcloth. Sometimes the leaders of new states ostentatiously follow traditional 'ways', as Dr Nkrumah does when he appears in public in a Ghanaian toga; this does not alter the fact that his relationship to the population of Ghana is something new in their history.

The entry into new relationships often involves disregard of pre-existing ones. People who have entered the large-scale society, as wage-earners, as cash farmers, as teachers, as politicians, often find that what is expected of them in their new role is incompatible with the expectations of their kinsmen or of traditional authorities. Those who remain within the limits of the small-scale society resent changes which work to their disadvantage, and may disapprove of the people who seize the new opportunities. There is a conflict of values; people have to weigh the loss of esteem in some quarters against the material or other advantages to be sought in new relationships. Other difficulties arise because people do not know how to foresee the consequences, or judge the advantages, of the choices they make in new situations. But the processes through which the changes of today are brought about are *the same* processes that maintained the small-scale societies in their relatively unchanging condition in the past: the pursuit of individual advantage within a framework of social expectations to which individuals respond by conformity or resistance, as they choose.

This interpretation of the contemporary process of social change in the underdeveloped territories may help to explain the difficulties met with in projects aimed at improving technical efficiency, whether in the field of production or that of welfare. It goes deeper than explanations of resistance to change in terms of attachment to traditional 'ways' or 'patterns', and it avoids some dangerous assumptions derived from theories of the persistence of 'patterns', such as the assumption that co-operation, or particular political forms, are 'naturally African'. Much of what is described as 'naturally African' is simply characteristic of the limited possibilities open to societies of simple technology.

This book tries to explain, in terms of the extension of the scale of social relationships, the characteristic changes that are taking place in the major social fields, and it has seemed pertinent to the explanation to examine also some current discussions of the general problem of social change.

LUCY MAIR

CHAPTER 1

NATIONS REMADE

'Small-scale' and 'Large-scale' societies—Change in social structure—The crucial techniques—Sources of Western influence—Characteristics of small-scale society—Characterisitic effects of Western influence.

THIS BOOK is an attempt to analyse a type of change in the structure of society that is taking place at the present time over a great part of the world. In those countries that are sometimes called 'under-developed' and sometimes, more hopefully, 'developing', determined attempts are being made to raise living standards by adopting productive techniques that were invented in the Western world. The leaders of these countries have set themselves to accelerate a process that was set in motion when the command of machine technology enabled its original possessors to extend their economic and political relationships all through the world, and to organise large-scale production in countries that did not themselves have the means to do this.

People who are not familiar with the work of social anthropologists may be surprised to find that this is a matter we are concerned with. We still have the reputation—which, of course, we made for ourselves in the past—of being concerned with 'primitive' peoples, and directing our interest to just those features of life in the developing nations that they themselves are anxious to get rid of. But this reputation refers to a period in the history of our studies which is now long distant. In the nineteenth century anthropology was expected to throw light on the primeval condition of man, and to explain how he moved from it to the condition of Western Europe and America at that time. Study was concentrated on such examples as could be found of the (relatively) 'untouched primitive', and on those aspects of their life that owed nothing to missionary teaching, the import of manufactured goods or the policies of colonising powers. Old men's memories of the past were considered the most valuable source of information.

But for a long time now social anthropologists have been interested in societies of simple technology, not for what they may lead us to guess about our own remote past, but for their own sakes. We are interested in the way they are organised for purposes of co-operation, and the way they keep this co-operation going and maintain respect for the rights and obligations that are recognised between their members.

This kind of interest leads in the first place to what is called a 'synchronic' study—a detailed study within a limited social field of the relationships existing at the time between the people under observation. The development of techniques for such study has been the major contribution of anthropology to the social sciences. The foundations of this kind of fieldwork were laid by Malinowski in his study of the Trobriands, a record so complete that it can be used today to answer questions that he never thought of.

Along with this change of emphasis from the remembered past to the observed present went a change in the type of interpretation of the data. The immediate predecessors of Malinowski explained social arrangements which seemed to them anomalous as 'survivals' of previous conditions of society in which they would have made more sense. Malinowski sought instead to see how these arrangements contributed to the maintenance of social co-operation, and, as he would have put it, the 'needs' of life in society, at the time when he was observing them. He had a sense of disillusionment with mechanised 'Western' society which many people shared and still share, and a sense of the duty of tolerance, and even respect, for alien institutions which I myself regard as the most important principle that anthropology can teach (I should add that it seems to be very easy for young people to graduate in social anthropology without acquiring this tolerance). These two attitudes combined with his love of paradox to make him idealise the conditions of Trobriand society, and argue that every change in it that was made in response to Western influence was for the worse, and it is perhaps to this more than anything that anthropologists owe their reputation for wanting to keep primitive people primitive. It is only fair to add that Malinowski did not maintain this position after he had travelled in Africa.

'Small-scale' and 'Large-scale' Societies

The central interest of the studies in Africa that were sponsored between the two world wars by the Rockefeller Foundation and the International African Institute was the nature of the changes that were taking place in African societies in response to Western influences. Today these changes would be epitomised in terms of the extension of the scale of social relationships, a mode of describing them that was first developed by two of Malinowski's pupils, Godfrey and Monica Wilson,[1] and this is how I shall look at them in this book. In the small-scale society of simple technology the field of people's relationships is confined, both physically because of the difficulties of travel, and socially in that the same persons and groups co-operate for all the important purposes of life. The large-scale society has at its disposal techniques of communication extending all over the world, and means of establishing impersonal relationships for specific transactions (notably by the use of money). Every member of the large-scale society is party to a great number of relationships, some ephemeral, some lasting, which do not overlap. Outside his immediate family he maintains few close bonds all through his life. This kind of loosely organised society, held together partly by impersonal transactions and partly by a great number of organisations for the pursuit of specialised ends and interests, contrasts strongly with the closely integrated village or kin-group that we find among peoples of simple technology.

When these latter are drawn into the world political and economic system, their individual members form new relationships outside the village and the kin-group, which often entail

1. *The Analysis of Social Change*, 1945

their physical separation from their kith and kin as well as making it difficult for them to fulfil all the obligations appropriate to the small-scale society. This is the process sometimes described as the disintegration of village life, and the word may often be appropriate when large numbers of the young men of a village leave it for work elsewhere. In contrast to the village, with its recognised physical form and established social order, the towns to which these young men go are new and strange and still largely inchoate. In the towns the necessary adaptation is gradually being made to the social relationships implicit in the large-scale society that modern techniques have created, and the disintegration of the old-style society of the villages is counter-balanced, for those who have successfully made the adjustment, by this integration into an urban society. This is perhaps a more accurate way of putting what Radcliffe-Brown has called the establishment of a new social equilibrium. He remarked that the process might take a long time.

It is certainly true that, just as a short time perspective may make an isolated small-scale society seem more unchanging than it really is, so it may lead to an unduly pessimistic view of one which is undergoing rapid change. Historians sympathetic to the new currents of opinion in the under-developed countries encourage us, by analogies from past experience elsewhere, to look forward to a happy outcome. But their time-span can lead to the opposite distortion. An anthropologist who sees the difficulties of adjustment as the cost that has to be paid for the raising of living standards cannot help giving a good deal of sympathy to the individuals who are paying the cost and will not live to enjoy the gain. This cannot be called, as it has often been, seeking to deny the benefits of progress to peoples whose way of life we want to preserve for our aesthetic satisfaction. Whatever may have been the attitude of a past generation of anthropologists, the romantic view of primitive life is now found less among them than among literary dilettantes who know little of it at first hand.

However, it is safer to avoid trying to distinguish between healthy and unhealthy conditions of society, to recognise that no society has ever been without its problems and dissatisfactions, and to note that in the conditions of particularly rapid change through which the tropical countries are passing today, a number of situations arise which either are not provided for in the accepted rules of a society or in which too many people are willing to disregard the rules that were accepted in the past. This is the aspect of the modern development of small-scale societies which attracted most attention at the time when their happiest future seemed to be in a gradual advance with plenty of time for readjustment. Now people are more concerned with resistance to plans for rapid change. These are two sides of the same situation.

Change in Social Structure

The kind of social change that is of interest to a student of society is the kind that he can see or trace occurring. And from the point of view of social theory, this kind of social change is interesting, not because it illustrates *different* social processes from those to be seen in what we may call a conservative society, but because it illustrates *the same* ones. It is the contention of this book that the social pressures which operate in a rapidly changing society are those which are to be found in any society, and are the same as those that maintain social institutions in being. If this statement seems like a paradox, it is because too little allowance is still made for the free play of personal choice which exists in the simplest societies. In *Crime and Custom in Savage Society* Malinowski wrote of the forces that make it difficult for the members of any society to depart too far from established norms; but he also showed how there is room for people to pursue their personal advantage by choosing between different permissible courses of action. The circumstances that this century has brought to the small-scale societies offer many new alternatives, all of which involve some departure from the standards of behaviour that were previously accepted, and thus the risk of incurring social disapproval. Some people think it worth their while to run this risk, others do not. Their attitudes depend on their ability to judge the situation and on whether they have more to gain by seizing new opportunities or by keeping to the old ways; gain being measured, as it has always been measured, in wealth, power, physical comfort and the esteem of one's neighbours. Different reactions to new opportunities are the reflection of differences in personality and in social status.

What is interesting to the social anthropologist is not change in items of behaviour but change in the totality which we call the social structure. The conception of a structure in society is one that does not occur spontaneously to the layman. Durkheim warned his readers that all the ways of thinking to which they were most accustomed would prove to be a hindrance rather than a help in the scientific study of society as he understood this. Marxists are indeed familiar with the idea of a class structure in which all the significant divisions of society are defined by their relationship to the means of production; but whatever the validity of this analysis for societies of complex technology, it is not easy to apply it to those which practise a subsistence economy. The popular unreflecting 'intuitive' picture of society is one of an aggregate of individuals each acting according to his or her own nature—overlaid sometimes with notions of 'racial' or 'national' characteristics which are supposed to lead all the members of large populations to act alike. This is due in part to the fact that the existence, if not the content, of psychological theories has received much wider recognition than has that of theories of society; it is interesting that many students take up anthropology because they think it will give them an insight into exotic mental processes. But another reason is that the common-sense view of human nature is built up by the direct experience of dealings with persons whom we think of simply as individuals, and extended mainly by works of fiction in which again—and rightly—the characters are of interest primarily for their individual reactions to the situations described. In any good novel the social pressures—the influences that are brought to bear on people through their membership of social groups—are there, but they do not obtrude themselves.

What makes a society something more than an aggregate of persons is the fact that, at any given moment, the appropriate relationships between its members are defined. It is when these relationships change that we can speak of social change. Social changes are very often the concomitants or consequences of technological changes, and in the field to be covered by this book, they are very largely so. Since technology is an aspect of culture, students of 'acculturation' and students of social change are looking at the same complex of events; but where the former might focus their attention on the 'acceptance' or 'rejection' of the printing-press by peoples who had not invented it, or the geographical path of its diffusion, the latter would be more interested in the way printing widens the range of communication.

There are not many societies which change so fast that there is not a recognisable structure into which children grow up. This may be the case in countries which have experienced a violent and successful revolution; and it may be the case with the populations of recent immigrants on the fringe of rapidly growing towns. But it is generally true that a large part of every child's preparation for adult life consists in learning the behaviour that will be expected of him in different relationships—not only whom he must respect and with whom he may be familiar, but—much more important—on whom he has claims and who has claims on him. The key terms which anthropologists use to describe the position of an individual in a social structure are *status* and *role*. Status is essentially a matter of the relationship that is thought to be proper between any given persons. Such relationships may result from the unique position of an individual as a member of a body of kin in which he is parent to some, child to others, mother's brother to others; or from his position as a member of some category of persons for whom there is an appropriate relationship to all persons in some other category, as that between men and women, seniors and juniors, persons of high and low rank. The sum of all the relationships in which he is involved is a person's status. The actual behaviour which is expected of him is his role.

In societies of simple technology status is largely determined by birth (*ascribed*). Rank is always, and political authority often, hereditary. Property rights depend on kinship, and within kin groups seniority gives authority and often the right to manage common property. In some societies relative age is made a principle of organisation, so that contemporaries have special obligations of mutual aid, and are expected to show formal deference to members of senior groups and entitled to claim this from members of junior groups. Some opportunities exist for pursuing personal advantage and ambition by entering into new relationships; of these marriage, which is a form of alliance, is the commonest. Perhaps the most striking difference between societies of simple and those of advanced technology is in the range of choice of relationships which is offered in the latter.

Sir Henry Maine, writing of ancient law, contrasted the importance of status in ancient societies with that of contract in modern ones. He was using the terms in the strictly legal sense, but anthropologists have taken over his phrase as a neat description of the characteristic changes which the simpler societies are experiencing today.

It is possible also to classify societies very broadly in terms of their techniques. From the point of view of the present study the techniques which are significant are those which are crucial for the extension of the range of social relationships. One can put the same statement in a negative form and say that what gives their special characteristics to the societies that we call 'simple' or 'small-scale' is the absence of these techniques.

The Crucial Techniques
The first of these is writing. So significant is this that some anthropologists have used the word 'pre-literate' to describe the essential characteristic of the societies that they study. Where writing is not known, the range of communications, and so of the giving of orders, is limited to that over which messages can be carried by word of mouth, and their effectiveness depends upon the safe arrival, the memory and the honesty of the messenger. In the economic field writing makes possible accurate records of claims and payments, and the making of inventories: it seems that the oldest examples of writing are

concerned with such matters, and not with religious mysteries or products of the imagination.

Pre-literate societies also lack money in the sense of a generally accepted medium of exchange. This is one reason why, in such societies, there are few impersonal economic transactions. Sometimes even the bartering of local products—pots from villages where there are clay deposits, fish from the sea coasts—depends on the existence of personal relationships between the individuals exchanging their goods. Markets where anyone can trade may, however, be found in societies without a cash economy. It is in the field of claims on services, and rewards for services given, that the contrast with the Western commercial economies is most marked. There is no such thing as the hiring at a fixed rate of anyone who offers his labour. A man owes services to his senior kinsman, or his future father-in-law, or the chief of his country, and the latter owes him a reward the amount of which lies in his discretion. Societies organised on this basis are, then, both pre-literate and pre-commercial.

The great empires of the east did not have to wait for Europe to bring them either literacy or commerce. But within these empires, as everywhere in the world throughout the greater part of its history, production was still organised on a small scale and peasant communities still lived largely self-contained lives. Robert Redfield distinguished between the wholly self-contained 'folk community' and the peasant community, which is a population living on the land, but linked to a town in that its produce is marketed there, that it may obtain some of its necessities there, and that it is governed by some official situated there. Peasants may go to the town with produce or may be obliged to go there to have legal cases settled, but their links with it are on the periphery of a life which is still centred in the village. Government is concerned mainly with the maintenance of law and order, the collection of tax or tribute, and perhaps the organisation of labour for public works such as those which controlled the flood waters of the great rivers of China.

This description, which today may call India or China to mind, would have applied to the whole of Europe two hundred years ago. The factor which has revolutionised Western civilisations is, of course, the invention of power-driven machinery. If the West can be said to have succeeded in digesting its revolution, this is because the new inventions were made one by one, and the process of reorganisation which was necessary in order to take advantage of the opportunities they offered proceeded gradually; at any rate the word can be used if we are comparing the history of the past two centuries in Europe and America with that of the past eighty years in Africa and Asia. Western political and economic penetration of these continents brought with it a fully-fledged machine technology to which their populations had to be induced or compelled to adjust themselves—sometimes, though not always, by alien rulers. Now that these countries have re-asserted their independence, it is their own ruling classes who are seeking to speed the process.

In contrasting small-scale and industrialised societies I have made the nature of the techniques at their disposal the essential characteristic which distinguishes them. It would be going too far to say that every feature of Western society is determined by the fact that it depends upon large-scale production; for example, there are differences between the political systems of industrialised countries which cannot be explained in terms of their economic systems. But there are two special reasons for insisting on this point in a discussion of contemporary social change in the tropics. One is that undoubtedly the entry of his country into the world economic system is what has made the biggest changes in the life of the tropical peasant. The other is that if we see advances in civilisation in terms of the development of techniques, we are less likely to think of Western society as having a way of life which is morally superior because of some moral superiority in persons of European descent. One can make a case for the moral superiority of *some*, by no means all, of the values of Western society. But one is driven back on the fact that it is technical equipment— yes, even in the Greek city-state—which enables people to cultivate the spirit of rational inquiry, which makes it intelligent to avoid causing physical pain as soon as pain ceases to be the inevitable human lot, and which makes it necessary for machine-workers to 'develop habits of regular labour' if the machines are to earn a return on the capital invested in them. It is, in the first place, our possession of writing that has enabled us to pursue consecutive arguments over long centuries, to re-interpret and to question dogmas, and thus to think critically about social institutions instead of taking them for granted. It is the control of the environment which the application of scientific principles to production has given us that makes it practicable for us to ask what is to be regarded as the good life, and how society should be organised to secure this for its members. This is something worth having, but we should not suppose that it is the product of special qualities implanted in us by nature.

Sources of Western influence
One can see the needs of commerce and large-scale production as the prime motive for the extension of European rule over tropical territories, as it is for the tightening of government control in those which remain independent. But the process of government does not consist entirely in furthering the spread of commerce. The most elementary function of government is to secure respect for law. Law itself is a body of rules of conduct collectively recognised by the members of any society, and believed by them to be a part of the moral order. Most agents of European authority believe as naïvely as their subjects do that the legal rules which they have been brought up to respect, and also the methods by which they are used to seeing these rules enforced, are the *only* right rules and the *only* true justice. Hence they impose these for other than interested reasons, and sometimes in fields where the interests of their own nations are little concerned.

Moreover, the socially constructive activities which modern governments are expected to undertake have been regarded as part of their function in their tropical dependencies as well. This again has led them to be active in promoting social change in other fields than those where the requirements of the new economic system call for it. Public health policies are the most conspicuous example of this kind of activity. Another question for governments, which is economic in nature though it is not always closely concerned with the development of the modern large-scale economy, is how to control the laws and practices involved in the use of land so that it shall, if possible, be made more productive, and at least not rendered useless by methods of cultivation which destroy fertility or even remove the top soil itself.

Yet another type of influence is that of missionaries, who have sought from genuinely disinterested motives to spread Christianity both in colonial and in independent territories. The first education, and the first medical work, of Western type which the peoples of these territories have received has often come from missionaries. It is common for missionaries to regard their message as comprising the whole value system of the society to which they belong. Thus they sometimes teach their converts that it is right for them to remain subordinate to Europeans, and they have much more often attacked social institutions, particularly those relating to marriage and the family, which were appropriate to the circumstances of the people among whom the missionaries worked and did not have the evil intentions or consequences that were ascribed to them. Yet they have been genuinely devoted to the welfare of these peoples as they saw it; have been, through their educational work, the means of preparing them to make their way in the Western world before governments had taken much responsibility for this; and have often spoken up in criticism of government policies which seemed to them to be contrary to the principles of Christian ethics or social justice. Missionaries in the Belgian Congo first called their government's attention to the effects on African village life of the recruiting of men in large numbers to work in mines and on plantations. The history of the 'political missionaries' in South Africa, from John Philip and John Mackenzie in the early nineteenth century to Michael Scott and Trevor Huddleston today, is a better-known example.

The direct influence of mission activity on social structure has been felt principally in the field of marital and family relations, since it is there that missionaries have felt most strongly that they must introduce radical changes. But the influences that are leading, in peasant societies, to the development of the close-knit domestic family, largely isolated from other kin and free to act independently of them, are to be found as much as in the general economic situation as in the teaching of missionaries.

Before following out in detail some of the changes that are taking place in particular aspects of the life of small-scale societies, we should consider more closely what can be seen as characteristic of the organisation of these societies, and at what points the adoption by them of Western techniques makes it necessary for this organisation to change.

Characteristics of Small-scale Society

The essential principles of organisation of small-scale societies are two: *kinship* and *membership of a territorial group*. Any recognisable territorial unit will usually have some identifiable authority, though this may be a body of persons and not a single individual, so that it is generally accurate to equate territorial with *political* structure. There are some cases of people who occupy a defined territory within which they recognise principles of orderly co-operation, but yet do not recognise any one person or persons as possessing authority over them all. The way in which such peoples maintain a sufficient degree of order to carry on social life is a question of great interest for the student of society, but for our purposes they are so exceptional that there is no need to examine them closely.

As a rough generalisation we may say that in small-scale societies people depend, to make their living and their way through life, primarily on co-operation with the family, which may be a 'joint' family of adult brothers with their wives and unmarried children; for assistance in economic activities which are part of the normal cycle, on their neighbours; for rights to property, and often for the defence of these rights, on their kinsmen, and on the recognised system of descent, whatever this may be, that prescribes the lines by which inheritance passes, and the people who are entitled to share in it. Where there is a centralised political system of the type which we are accustomed to recognise as a state, people receive, in return for subordination to political authorities, protection of their persons and property against their neighbours and against external enemies. With the development of such systems goes economic differentiation. Rulers have recognised claims on the wealth and the labour of their subjects, and from the resources which they are able to accumulate they can reward their followers and so secure their loyalty. Even in the smallest societies so organised, such as the Ngwato of Bechuanaland with a population of 101,000 or the Lozi of Northern Rhodesia with 140,000 (I give the numbers as they were when the available anthropological accounts of these societies were made), there was room for the play of ambition and the pursuit of advancement through the favour of superior authorities, advancement gained through general loyalty to the superior or by specific qualities such as success in war or skill in settling legal cases. The incentives to ambition, therefore, were such as tended to reinforce the social order.

The scene of most discussion about political authority in small-scale societies has been African, because all the European governments which have established themselves in Africa have had to decide whether or not they should recognise African rulers, and, if they did, what should be the extent of the authority left to them. Nineteenth-century liberals, with their certainty that all authority which was not subject to popular control must be tyrannous, saw them merely as petty despots, and indeed there are well-authenticated stories of the ferocious punishments meted out by African rulers to disobedient subjects; the ancient crocodile to whom the unfaithful wives of the Ganda king were thrown was still being shown to visitors not so many years ago.

The maintenance of the kingly state was often held to involve the taking of human life, sometimes on a large scale, as at the funerals of Akan chiefs in Ghana, when their followers were expected to accompany them to the other world. It is true too that the claims of rulers on the wealth of their subjects were either not fixed or fixed at a very high level.

In practice this was not often regarded as a reason for eliminating hereditary rulers from the political scene, and when their position began to be challenged the argument was put forward that they are more democratic than was at first supposed. Among a few peoples there are named institutions with recognised procedures for getting rid of an authority who does not act in the manner expected of him. An example which one often hears quoted is that of the Yoruba chiefs, for whom to receive a present of a parrot's egg was a sign that it was time to quit the mortal scene. It has, however, been remarked in this context that putting the black spot on a pirate king may be an effective way of expressing dissatisfaction, but is hardly a democratic one.

It is an abuse even of that so much abused word 'democracy' to apply it to any and every mitigation of absolute despotism. But the fact is that absolute despotism is a rather rare phenomenon. How far any ruler can go contrary to the expectations of his subjects depends ultimately upon how much force he has at his disposal. This depends, first, on his being able to secure a following of persons whose prime loyalty is to him and not to some one section of the society (their own kinsmen for example), and secondly on the type of weapons at his disposal. If, as is the case in the small-scale societies, the ruler's bodyguard is armed with no better weapons than those in the possession of every citizen, his preponderance of power is not great.

In African as in any other society, government was conceived to be for the benefit of the governed, though there might be second-class citizens, slaves or serfs, whose interests were held to be of small account. There was in fact a reciprocal relationship between rulers and ruled, some aspects of which have been mentioned. Defence against enemies, and above all success in attacks upon them, were recognised as benefits; still more so was a judicial system which relieved individuals of the necessity of fighting for their rights. It is on record that the Alur people of Western Uganda were able to extend their power over their less well-organised neighbours because the latter would come to some chief and petition him to give them one of his sons 'to settle our disputes for us'. The stores collected in tribute might serve, in the first place, to reward the ruler's own followers, but they had other public purposes as well. They enabled him to make feasts for the men who came to work on his fields or build his capital; in Buganda old men think of this as one of the pleasures of doing this work, outweighed though it might be by the risk of incurring condign punishment for some misdemeanour. They enabled him to assist his subjects in distress—a general disaster such as famine or a personal disaster such as the loss of all one's cattle. The Lozi custom was that whenever a load of tribute was brought to the royal court, a proportion of it was set apart to be distributed among all who were in the place at the time. Finally, most African rulers were believed to have ritual functions which only they could perform; in many cases these were associated with the control of rain—securing both that it should fall at the right time and that it should not fall at the wrong. If there are proverbs and sayings about the dread nature of kingship, its absolute power, and so on, there are many others which describe rulers as fathers and guardians of their people, with the duty of 'cherishing' them. Ceremonies of accession emphasised the duties of the chief to his people as well as theirs to him.

There were also more effective checks on the abuse of authority than feelings and words. It is of the nature of hereditary rule that there are rival claimants to succession. This is so however much the rules may seem to designate one person and one only. What if it can be argued that the mother of the heir apparent was not legally married? Englishmen know some of the consequences in their own history. African systems allowed many more occasions of dispute. There was usually a rival claimant who could build up support against an unpopular chief, though it is interesting that in Africa the way out of an intolerable situation was found on the whole more often through secession than through rebellion. A person of high status could move off taking his followers with him. If he was powerful enough, and far enough from the centre of power, he could simply proclaim his independence by refusing to pay tribute; if he was not quite powerful enough he might have to seek safety by transferring his allegiance to another powerful ruler. For the ordinary peasant escape was harder; he probably could not leave his tribe altogether, but he could often move within it from the area of authority of one territorial official to that of another. Since for all persons in authority wealth and power depended on the numbers of those subject to them, there were strong arguments for ruling in a way that would attract rather than repel subjects. This only very approximately secures general contentment. The last proposition is also true of any system of representative government, but some kind of representative government is a necessary part of the organisation of political units on a large scale.

Characteristic Effects of Western Influence

Looked at from the point of view of the agent of Westernisation, whether or not himself a native of a Western country, the major changes which this process calls for can be classified as either economic or political. Certain types of economic and certain types of political re-organisation are necessary in order to make it possible to take advantage of Western scientific and mechanical techniques. But from the point of view of the people who are called on to make the changes they cannot be compartmentalised in this way. The economic changes in particular affect every relationship in the small-scale society.

These changes were introduced in the first place by people in direct pursuit of profit for themselves, and animated by little regard for the interests of the societies among which they might be operating. In the early days of gold and diamond mining in South Africa, and of plantations in the Pacific, it would be hard to say that the demand for labour among people who at that time, since they did not know what money could do, were not interested in leaving their homes to earn it, brought them anything to compensate for the disorganisation of what had previously been an organised existence. It did not *in itself* do anything towards that suppression of internecine warfare which is claimed as the earliest benefit of European rule. Indeed, since the first object which African labourers at

Kimberley usually bought with their earnings was a gun, the contrary might be said to be true in that case.

If the days of blackbirding in the Pacific are now long past, those of the three-year labour contract, breach of which was punished as a crime, are more recent. The effects of the un-regulated recruiting of labourers who were bound by contracts of this type make an unhappy chapter in the history of the economic development of the tropics. They led some humani-tarians—not all of them anthropologists by any means—to argue that this had brought nothing but harm to the indigenous peoples and would have been better left undone. This is the view that has been commonly misrepresented as 'trying to preserve tropical territories as anthropological zoos'.

Professor Arthur Lewis has remarked that today the imagin-ary exponents of this view are crying for the moon. It is cer-tainly true that today there is nowhere any need to put pressure on Africans or Pacific Islanders to go long distances from their homes to earn wages, and in so far as the consequences of this are socially unsatisfactory, the remedy must be sought by some other means than trying to put the clock back.

The characteristic feature of labour in the countries we are considering is that it is *migratory*. The labour force required particularly for mining, but also for plantation agriculture, for any kind of construction work, in docks and on railways, is never available close at hand. It is only modern economic development that enables populations to live in the close con-centration that this would imply. Hence labourers have had to come from a distance. They came as single men, leaving their families behind and returning when they had saved enough from their earnings, or, if they had signed a contract, when they had completed this. This system, a product of the em-ployers' necessity, was at first justified by the assumption that in any case the young men did no work when they were at home. Actually, it withdrew necessary manpower from village agriculture and often resulted in a reduction in the food-supply for which their money earnings did not compensate.

Today it is realised in most countries that industrial develop-ment necessarily implies greater specialisation and the division

28

of the population into full-time industrial workers and commercial farmers, and the policy of some governments is actively directed towards this end. But it is still far from having been attained.

In certain regions it has been found practicable for peasant farmers to grow saleable crops and so earn money incomes without leaving their homes. In these cases social change takes different forms, of which perhaps the most important is the development of new relationships arising out of rights in land. In an economy where nothing is bought or sold, it is obvious that land cannot be, and in a society with such an economy rights to cultivate land depend not on purchase or the payment of rent, but either on membership of a kin group, on allegiance to a political authority, or on a special personal relationship with a right-holder.

As soon, however, as there is competition for land, either because land as such is scarce or because there is a keen demand for particular land, such as the rain forest land where alone cocoa will grow, or land in the narrow 'fertile crescent' of Uganda close to Lake Victoria, people who have rights in it learn that their rights can be made a source of income. In the dependent territories this process has rarely been allowed to work itself out unhindered. Governments have been afraid to allow peasants to dispose freely of land rights for fear they should get into debt and lose their land while they had no other source of livelihood. In the territories which have made respect for local custom a principle of administration, it has always been difficult to judge the point at which this custom, with its insistence on group control over the disposal of land, can be said to have become obsolete. On the other hand, in territories which have attached more importance to the rapid introduction of Western institutions, it has sometimes happened that the whole territory of a village or even a tribe has been allocated in individual tenure before any demand had arisen for the right of free disposal of land.

Yet another consequence of the cultivation of cash crops has been considerable immigration into the regions where this is most profitable, and this results in problems of the extent to which immigrants will be accepted as members of the community in possession of the territory, which are no less acute than the corresponding ones in Western countries.

These are direct effects of turning subsistence cultivators into wage-earners or cash farmers. The indirect effects of introducing a money economy into societies where it was new, and even to some extent of increasing the opportunities for earning money incomes in societies where money was already circulating, have been all-pervading. To understand their force we must recognise that the transfer of articles of value between members of a non-commercial society has quite a different significance from what it has where goods are exchanged against cash. Comments by early missionaries on African marriage ceremonies often emphasise the fact that at every step of a bride's journey to her husband's house and her entry into it, she demanded payment from her husband. This, and still more the general practice of handing over cattle or other valuables from the bridegroom's family to that of the bride, were held to be the expression of a sordidly commercial attitude towards a human relationship which should be sacred. It would not be too paradoxical to say that only people accustomed to a society in which almost the whole of life is conducted in terms of commercial transactions could interpret in this way the significance of gifts and giving in non-commercial societies. For them the making of gifts is an inseparable part of the creation of any new relationship; it not only makes the event memorable, and so takes the place of a written record, but the gift itself creates the new tie by bringing two persons into the relationship of giver and receiver. In the case of marriage it can certainly be argued that the cattle transfer is a return to the bride's people for their gift of her to her husband, *provided it is understood that a return is not a payment, nor a payment a price.* We pay respects, compliments, homage, visits, after all. In a non-commercial society people return gift for gift, and they reward specific economic services, or more intangible ones such as political loyalty, *but they do not pay for these things.* What is the essential difference? That, though the reward or return gift is due, it cannot be claimed; to make it is a moral and not a contractual obligation. A certain equivalence may be expected, but it cannot be insisted upon. Even the cattle transfer at marriage, with all the discussion that may precede it, where the number of beasts to be handed over is fixed by agreement of the two parties and where claims at law may arise over failures to produce them, belongs to another world than that of commercial dealings. These payments have to be thought of as a series of linked transactions in which cattle circulate endlessly along the lines formed by specific kinship ties: one of the factors which keep the whole network of these ties in being is the expectation of receiving cattle from particular persons on the occasion of particular marriages. Nothing could be further from the discontinuous transactions, each complete in itself, that we call buying and selling. It would be going too far to say that in any given society, unless everything is bought and sold, nothing is; for in Western society there are still small corners in which social relationships are created and maintained by gift and counter-gift (including, as in small-scale societies, hospitality as a form of gift). But I offer this as a rough description of the contrast between commercial and noncommercial societies.

If this book may seem to be unduly concerned with what is happening in African societies, I must plead that this has been the preoccupation of the greater part of my academic life. But the processes that I describe can be traced everywhere that Western technology has penetrated, and I have given such examples from outside Africa as a non-specialist in other fields can find. If I am held to have erred in bringing the oriental world under the heading 'new nations', I would say that in this century its ancient nations have assuredly been made new.

CHAPTER 2

NEW MODES OF LIVELIHOOD

Disruption of village economy—Wage-labourers—Cash farmers—Cash expenditures—Land rights—Sources of credit.

WHATEVER ASPECT of social structure is considered, it will be found that the most striking changes can be seen as the effects of the introduction or wider extension of a money economy and the development of large-scale industry. But some changes in those social relationships are more closely concerned than others with economic affairs. The wider relationships involved in large-scale commerce and industry are focused in the urban centres which new developments have either created or greatly enlarged, and it is there that the new social groups which they have called into being are growing up. The social structure of these towns is affected only a little by the rural background of their new populations, and is better discussed by itself as something which is being created rather than experiencing change. The subject of this chapter is the effect of Western influences on economic organisations in the rural areas.

What this is depends upon the form in which new economic opportunities present themselves. The crucial question is whether a cash income can be obtained by farming. If it can, the developments that we have to consider concern rights in land and the organisation of cultivation, the extension of trading relations and the provision of credit. The extension of the field of trade is something that economists but not sociologists have studied. In Nigeria, for example, we know that the women who from time immemorial have taken their small surpluses to market travelled farther and farther afield as means of transport became easier, and that today some women dealers in the market of Onitsha may buy and sell a thousand pounds' worth of goods in a day and dispatch them by lorry all over the country. But we know less than we would like about the organisation that this must involve, or the status of the ladies who have this economic achievement to their credit. This development is only one example of the ways in which new sources of gain can be exploited so that inequalities of wealth become far wider than anything these societies had known before. The possessors of large incomes use them to adopt a way of life that in its material aspects at least is modelled on that of the West; and this, along with the appearance of new professions and salaried employments, leads to the differentiation of society even in the rural areas.

Another new social development about which we still know too little is the deliberate creation of new communities where settlement has been organised by governments, either in connection with migration schemes or where scattered populations have been concentrated in villages and land holdings consolidated. Yet another field in which the process of change has nowhere been clearly traced—and nearly everywhere it is now too late to do so—is the effect on economic organisation of the suppression of slavery.

Wage-Labourers

In societies that depend for cash incomes on the emigration of wage-earners to centres of employment, what is of interest from the point of view of the home base in the rural area is the nature of this migration—who takes part in it, how long do they stay away, what do they in fact contribute to the home economy and how are necessary economic activities affected by their absence?

In most rural areas in the recently industrialised countries, at any given time a number of the younger men are away from home earning money, and their earnings have come to be taken for granted as part of the village economy; but the villagers still expect to get their food supply direct from their own lands in the traditional way. The manpower available for this is depleted in just the proportion that it is diverted to the earning of cash. The goods that can be bought with cash are goods that could not be produced in the village; but if the production of food in the village suffers through the loss of manpower, this is not made up for by the cash or goods that the labourers contribute to the village economy. This is a situation in which it is hard to balance gain and loss. We commonly think of the possession of a wider range of goods as signifying an improvement in standards of living; we think of a reduction in the food supply as signifying a deterioration. Not many of the villagers would forgo the goods for the sake of having more food; even the families which, in the end, find themselves in straits because their menfolk stay away too long may well have encouraged them in the beginning to go out and see what they could earn.

The introduction of wage labour to tropical territories has rarely been a matter simply of offering inducements. One could cite from Africa a few cases where populations had become familiar with trade goods before there was any demand for labour, and so readily left their homes to earn money when this opportunity offered. The tribes of Bechuanaland are one; men from there were seeking work on the Kimberley diamond mines before there was any organised recruiting of labour. More often, however, the advantages to be derived from a long sojourn in unaccustomed conditions in a strange and distant place were not obvious to the young men who were asked to undertake it, and pressure of various kinds was put upon them. Recruiting agents were not over-scrupulous in their methods of obtaining labour. Labourers were required to sign contracts binding them to work for fixed periods, and the breach of such a contract was treated as a criminal offence. In those parts of the world—the South Seas and South-East Asia in particular—where labourers were brought by sea to their place of work, the employers maintained that they could not recoup their expenses unless they could keep the men for three years, and in New Guinea, for example, the normal labour contract was for three years and could be renewed for another three. The story of the early period of the economic development of the tropics is not among the more edifying pages of history.

Today, however, it would not be wholly true anywhere, and in some places it would be quite untrue, to say that wage-labourers leave home only as a result of pressures other than that of the desire for a cash income. One form of pressure which certainly is significant is the liability to pay a tax to the government. This liability falls in some form or other on all subjects of organised government, and it is imposed to meet the cost of government. Although people in authority are sometimes on record as observing with gratification that the need to find the money for the tax has stimulated young men to seek employment, there are few cases where a tax has been imposed, or increased, with that end alone, and some governments have refused to use taxation in this way although employers of labour were urging them to do so. Also, there are now few, if any, cases in which people are not interested in money for any purpose except paying their taxes. At the same time, there are still many for whom the crucial consideration in deciding to go away to work at a particular moment is the fact that the tax is due, and can most easily be raised by accepting an advance on wages from a recruiting agency. On the other hand, some people have travelled long distances to seek employment before they were subject to any taxation at all.

If we look around Africa, we can see peoples in whose economy wages earned away from home play a greater or lesser part. It is the general experience that more and more trade goods come to be desired and eventually to be regarded as indispensable; so that we may legitimately consider these peoples as being at different stages of a general process. At one end are—or were some twenty years ago, when last an anthropologist looked at them closely—the Nuer of the southern Sudan, interested solely in their cattle and still procuring their total subsistence from their extraordinarily difficult environment. Next might come the Ngoni of Tanganyika, whose estimate of their necessities is low, but includes cotton clothing in place of the traditional skins. Other peoples are interested in ploughs, bicycles, electric torches, bedsteads, enamel basins and aluminium pots and pans.

This standard of necessities could be translated into cash terms as an annual income of so much. Indeed this calculation has been made for the Ngoni.[1] It does not anywhere reach, for a whole population, a level which would make it necessary for every man to work for wages all through his active life. Those individuals who do decide to adopt wage labour as their way of life move away from their home country to settle in some town. The rest depend on the periodical visits to centres of employment of the younger men, who are expected to help their parents as well as supporting their own wives and children.

In the early days of European administration in tropical territories it was assumed that men did no work but, not having attained to the chivalrous conception of womanhood characteristic of the middle classes in Europe, made their wives do it all. It is true that in most tropical countries, as in most peasant societies, women work very hard, and in addition to cooking have to fetch water and firewood and do a large part of the cultivation. It is also true that one of the traditional male activities—warfare—has been put an end to by the establishment of large-scale government, and another—hunting—has lost its importance in the economy. Nevertheless, there are times when young men are needed to work in the fields, notably when the ground is being prepared for sowing, and, particularly in those areas where ploughs are used, the shortage of manpower at this time may easily affect the food supply; either too little ground is cleared, or it is not cleared in time for the first rain.

Many of the men who go away to earn money realise that their labour will be missed at home, and try to arrange their journeys so as not to be away at the times when they are most needed. But this becomes more difficult as the amount which it is considered necessary to earn increases. In the early days of the Kimberley diamond mines Tswana labourers would not stay longer than four to six months. There are still some who try to be at home every year for the ploughing season, and

1. By Dr P. H. Gulliver, *Labour Migration in a Rural Economy*, 1955

more who make a point of doing their share at the busy time of year before they leave home—in some territories they are even compelled to stay—even though they do not come back the next year.

The Tanganyika Ngoni are able to meet their relatively low standard of cash needs if every man makes two journeys to work in his lifetime; most of them make the first before they are married, and many make both before they are thirty years old. They have another source of cash income in tobacco, which they can grow at home; this is less profitable, but the older men are content with it. But it may well be that their standards will rise, and they will follow a course similar to that of the Tswana tribes, with whom the total period spent at work, and the average period of continuous absence from home, is steadily increasing, while the time spent at home between periods earning wages is growing shorter. As this happens it becomes less and less practicable to dovetail the work of the farmer with that of the labourer. One reason for this development among the Tswana is the fact that they have very few local products which they can sell. Their total cash income, and therefore the total amount of goods possessed by the community, is thus higher than it could possibly be if the young men did not go away to work for wages. But of course everyone does not share equally in this; there may be families with no young sons, or the absentee may forget, or be unable, to send money home, or decide to stay in the town for good, forgetting old ties of kinship and forming new ones through marriage with foreign women.

The consequence can be seen most clearly in the state of cultivation. When only a minority of the men went away, some kinsman of the absent labourer was always available to help his wife with the ploughing; as the number away increases, so does the burden on those at home. Some fields are not ploughed at all, others too late in the season. Sometimes men who are away send money home for their wives to pay labour for ploughing; this employment of paid labour creates a new kind of social relationship which will have to be discussed more fully later.

In the Union of South Africa this process has gone even further. This is due in part to the steadily increasing demand for African labour. But a factor which is particularly important here is the extreme shortage of land for cultivation; this too is an element in the modern process of social change which will have to be considered by itself later. The area of land allotted to most of the African peoples of the Union is not large enough for every family to have a field to grow its own foodstuffs, let alone anything to sell; this situation has parallels in the most congested parts of other territories, but the Union is the extreme case. Of the Keiskammhoek district of the Cape Province it has been said that without the resource of wage labour the population would starve.[1] Here a large number of women as well as men spend their most active years away from their rural homes, and to an even greater extent the work of cultivation is left to the children and old people.

To persons responsible for the policies of governments the most distressing aspect of this situation is that agricultural resources are either not being developed or—more often—are being ruined by inefficient farming. Agricultural Departments train demonstrators to teach farming methods which would at least preserve the soil from the complete loss of its fertility and possibly make it more productive. But at any given time most of the energetic and intelligent potential farmers to whom their teaching should be addressed are away pursuing other avocations, and hardly anyone belonging to this section of the population expects to spend more time as a farmer than as a wage-earner. The care of cattle too is deteriorating, since herding has always fallen to the younger men; this is work that women and old men cannot do, so now it is left to boys. Indeed it may well be that work for wages is attractive partly because it is an alternative to the long spells of isolation at the distant posts where the Tswana cattle are herded when all the ground nearer the village is under crops; as in the case of a very different people, the cattle-owning Fulani of West Africa, where, although there is no necessity to seek employment, young men

1. D. H. Houghton and E. M. Walton, *The Economy of a Native Reserve*, 1952, p. 183

make of it an opportunity to get away from this arduous work.

From the point of view of economic efficiency, we must admit that among the peoples who have become dependent on migrant labour the response of the former subsistence farmer to new opportunities has led to unfortunate results. This is not due by any means entirely to the free choice of the labourers. Many employers have found it convenient to have a labour force of single men paid wages which did not take account of their dependent families, and governments have found it equally so to be absolved from responsibility for the support of unemployed labourers. It has suited them to think of the cash earnings of the labourers as a supplement to the subsistence economy of the rural area, on which they could always fall back in times of depression. Hence very little attempt has been made to induce Africans, or other tropical wage earners, to make a clean break with village life and adopt that of townsmen dependent wholly on their wages. Only the Belgian Congo government set itself seriously to do this. On the contrary, many governments have disliked what they sometimes call the 'detribalisation' of non-European peoples. In particular that of the Union of South Africa, the most thoroughly industrialised of the African countries, has consistently sought to oppose the permanent migration of Africans away from the land set aside for them. Yet the Africans' preferences also affect the situation. Though more and more of them do wish to become townsmen, there are still many who do not—who seek to keep a foot in both worlds, regarding the village as their home, retaining their rights in its land, having their children brought up there, and often going back after many years of absence when they have finally had enough of wage labour.

The subject of this book is not the problems of government policy but the changes in social relationships that the influence of Western industrial civilisation is bringing about. At this point we are concerned with changes in economic organisation. We see that a new division of labour has appeared, in which a family depends upon its younger men—that is the father at one stage, the sons at another—for a cash income which it cannot do without, but for its foodstuffs still on work of traditional type, done now by a smaller and less efficient labour force than was available for this purpose in the past. We see too that the traditional reliance on kinsmen to take the place of a man who is unable to carry out the tasks that should fall to him is no longer feasible. And here—as was mentioned earlier—we see the emergence of new contractual relationships by means of which necessary work gets done.

These arrangements are not always cash transactions. It has been noted that Tswana men may send money to their wives to pay for ploughing, as Cewa men in Nyasaland do to pay for having their houses kept in repair. But in other cases a woman will have a friend plough her field in return for her work later on in weeding or harvesting, or for a share of the crop. The latter arrangement is one of mutual convenience, for there may be men who have less land of their own than they could cultivate, and who by a share-cropping agreement in effect increase their own area under crops.

The last two instances are of people who cannot earn a cash income by farming. But there are many who, like the Ngoni of Tanganyika, have enough land to grow a cash crop and a market for their produce. For them there is a choice between staying at home and farming their land or earning the cash that they need in some employment that takes them away, and the choice is a matter of rational calculation based on the estimated difference in return, and taking into account the fact that a stipulated wage is paid regularly, whereas an independent farmer has to bear his own risks. For the Ngoni the calculation is fairly clear. What they can make by growing tobacco is less than they could earn by wage labour, but as they grow older they are content with a smaller income—which means, for practical purposes, wearing their clothes longer—and hope to get presents from time to time from their sons.

There are also people, such as the groundnut farmers of Northern Nigeria, who every year go south, after they have harvested their own crops, to work on the cocoa farms where the harvest comes later; and here we come to another of the significant new social relationships—the employment of wage labour by African cash-crop farmers.

Cash Farmers

Those who are in a position to employ others are, naturally, the fortunate peoples in whose country a profitable crop can be grown—cotton for the Ganda, coffee for the Chagga in Tanganyika, cocoa for the peoples of the rain-forest belt in West Africa—Yoruba, Akan, Agni and Bete. Their introduction to the world economic system has led to social changes of a very different kind from those which have been described up to now.

It is clear that if African farmers are to grow crops for sale as well as to eat they must cultivate a larger area than their fathers did. The naïve outsider's assumption is that this can be done by 'men working harder', and certainly there are cases—the Ganda provide one—where men who were not traditionally expected to do any farm work now do a good deal. But there are always peak periods which call for more manpower than a single household can provide: notably, of course, the harvest. The more a farmer shows enterprise in planting his land with cash crops, the more he is committed to finding extra labour when they have to be harvested. Moreover, the notion that one of the satisfactions that money can buy is exemption from the more arduous kinds of work is not confined to Europeans; though for some reason Europeans have deplored its spread to other peoples.

So the successful African farmer employs his own labourers, all the year round if he can, but at harvest time in any case. Plantations of tree crops such as coffee or cocoa have often been made in virgin forest, and in many cases the owners of the land have had it cleared by labourers. Once a plantation of this kind has been made, of course there is no question of annual clearing, but there is annual weeding, and for this too paid labour may be employed.

Examples have been given of arrangements by which women whose husbands are away may pay a neighbour to do a job of ploughing or thatching for them. These are agreements for a single piece of work. But it is characteristic of modern developments in African agriculture that people do not expect to enter into a continuing relationship of employer and employee with members of their own tribe. Here we may note that Maine's dichotomy between societies based on status and those based on contract cannot be accepted without any qualification. The relationship of employer and wage-earner is a contractual one, and the employer is not usually interested in the social status of his employees. But there are persons in every society who thinks their status makes it inappropriate for them to undertake certain kinds of work, and in agricultural societies where wage-labour is a new development it is unusual for people to work for wages in their own homes, perhaps because to do so is an admission that one cannot attain the status of an independent producer, perhaps simply because it would involve too radical a change in the accepted system of relationships. Both in Africa and in China, the labour employed for wages is drawn largely from areas outside the village where they are employed, and often from different peoples—in Uganda, Nigeria and Ghana from tribes outside the cash crop area, in China sometimes from the aboriginal hill peoples, or, if the labourers are Chinese, from other villages.

These immigrants are 'foreigners' in a truer sense than that in which the word has been used in English villages of newcomers from other parts of England. They speak a different language and are subjects of different chiefs and sometimes even of different states, like the immigrants into Uganda from the Congo or into Ghana from French-speaking countries. Some of them are migrants like the African migrant employees of European entrepreneurs. Others hope to settle in the richer country and become independent farmers. Sometimes this is made as difficult for them as it is made difficult for Africans to settle in the towns which Europeans have created.

One of these countries of immigration is the Buganda Province of Uganda, to which there comes a steady stream of labourers from Rwanda and Butundi, once the Belgian Trusteeship Territory, and a smaller number from the interior of Uganda itself and from western Kenya.[1] They are eagerly welcomed both by African and non-African employers. What is

1. See A. I. Richards, ed., *Economic Development and Tribal Change*, n.d.

of interest to the student of social change are the terms on which they undertake to work for the former.

Much of the work done is of the odd-job type, a day or two for a number of different employees in turn. Sometimes the labourers work simply for their food, at other times a payment for a fixed task, such as an area of land to be cleared, is agreed on after hard bargaining. This kind of work appeals mainly to young unmarried men, bands of whom build little camps of grass huts and go out to work together. The same people can dovetail spells of work for money and work for food.

Other men work for a single employer for regular wages. These are employed partly in agriculture and partly in tasks which would otherwise fall to the women of the household, such as fetching water and firewood. Their duties are very much the same as those which in the old days fell to the lot of men captured in war and made slaves, and the change in Ganda society that is most worthy of note in this context is the change in the circumstances which enable people to command this extra manpower. War captives seem to have been distributed with other loot, after a victory, among the men who had taken part in the fighting, on two principles: that a good fighter deserved some reward, and that the spoils of war were a source from which the ruler conferred favour on those of his subjects who were conspicuously loyal. Today a Ganda may be in a position to employ labour because he is a successful farmer, because he is a landowner (a special feature of Ganda society to be mentioned later), or because he holds a position in the political hierarchy for which he receives a cash salary. Very few employ a large labour force.

Whereas the labourers who seek employment in European concerns look solely to their wages for a cash income, the immigrants to Buganda often combine casual labour with the cultivation of a patch of cotton; the proceeds of this may be worth more than what they earn in wages, and the latter may be only a means of tiding over while they wait for the crop to ripen.

In order to grow such a crop they must of course be able to arrange for the use of land with someone who controls the disposal of land. The question how the exercise of rights in land is affected by the possibility of turning it to commercial use is a large one, which will have to be dealt with at length in its place. In the present context what is interesting is that the payment made for cultivation rights is not a money rent but a share of the yield—one bag, or two bags, of the cotton harvested. Of course it may be the cash value of this that is actually handed over.

In West Africa it is the cocoa farms of the Western Region of Nigeria, Ghana and the Ivory Coast which attract labourers from less fortunate parts, and here too some of the labourers are prospective settlers, while others come for short periods to earn a cash income at the time of year when there is little work to be done on their own food crops at home. Their work is needed not only when the cocoa has to be plucked and prepared for market by drying and fermenting the beans, and taken to the buyer, but also sometimes for weeding, and very frequently for new planting, which involves the clearing of virgin forest.

In Ghana, where a careful study has been made of the organisation of cocoa farming,[1] there is even more variety in the types of arrangement that are made between employers and labourers than there is in Buganda. As in Buganda, some work by the day and some by the task; some also engage to work for a year with one employer. This last class is mainly employed in cleaning, planting and weeding new cocoa farms; their employers give them food, tools and working clothes, and sometimes also housing, and so can reasonably claim their whole working time. These are mainly migrant labourers in the strict sense of the word, with homes elsewhere which they do not intend to leave.

An intermediate type is the man who is paid for the work he does on a cocoa farm by a sum fixed in advance for each bag of cocoa which he plucks, prepares and carries to market. Such a man may come to the cocoa belt for the crop season only, or may spend the greater part of his time there, occasionally going back to his home, or he may have his family with him and in

1. *See* Polly Hill, *The Gold Coast Cocoa Farmer*, 1956

that case may attach himself to one employer; then he will be expected to weed the farm as well as harvest the cocoa. He may work for more than one farmer, or supplement his cocoa work with other earnings. If he proposes to bring his family his employer will give him a house and land to grow his and their food. Arrangements of this type are confined to limited areas, and appear to be associated with the migration of the employers themselves from one centre, Akwapim. One cannot guess how any one way of rewarding labour originated, but it is interesting to see how one may come to be regarded as the obviously right way simply because it has been the practice of a particular area.

The most interesting arrangement is that which gives the labourer a share in the crop, so that his position approximates to that of a tenant of the chief. Indeed in Ghana arrangements of this type are popularly associated with those by which, as in Buganda, an independent farmer obtains the right to cultivate land on condition of handing over a part of the crop to the landowner (who in Ghana is the chief). The same word, *abusa*, which connotes division into three, is used of the tenant farmer's payment to the chief of a third of the crop and of the labourer's right to a third of it in return for his labour. The first *abusa* labourers were employed to clear and plant up new cocoa farms. They might be paid cash wages during the period before the trees came into bearing, but sometimes the labourer simply offered to make a new farm on the understanding that he would be entitled to a third of the crop as long as he looked after the farm. This was measured, not in bags of cocoa but in numbers of trees, or area, plucked; he was actually acquiring a small farm for himself in return for clearing and tending a larger area for someone else.

Now it is normal in some areas for the owners of farms to have all the cultivation work done by *abusa* labourers, themselves only supervising the work. This enables some of them to pursue other avocations, and it also makes it possible for the same man to have several farms some distance apart. If at one time the farmer with his family worked the original farm, leaving it to the *abusa* man with his to make the new plantation, today the *abusa* men and their families are the whole labour force in the areas where this system prevails.

A development that has been noticed across the frontier among the Agni of the Ivory Coast is that members of different peoples are employed for different kinds of work other than argiculture—some dig wells, others build houses. Little bands of men from Savalou in Dahomey travel through the country stopping where they are offered employment as builders. In Ghana there are large numbers of building contractors operating on a small scale, and all over West Africa there are small entrepreneurs owning lorries or buses. No study has been made of the composition of their labour force: doubtless it would be found that it consists of immigrants to the area where they are employed.

Cash Expenditures
What do the possessors of a money income do with it? We have seen that most African peoples now have a standard of necessities, however simple, which cannot be met without a cash income, even though the amount required may be very small. But in the more fortunate times and places there are people who earn enough to have a margin for expenditure over and above necessities. To a large extent these people emulate the patterns of consumption that are set by the Europeans who initiated them into the money economy. This often leads Europeans to regard them as extravagant, squandering their money as it comes instead of prudently saving it. Moreover, they also spend money in directions where Europeans would not spend it, notably in the feasts associated with marriage, and, after a death, with the end of mourning, and this Europeans regard as even more extravagant. Indeed in some tropical territories Europeans have encouraged the founding of 'better living' societies, the members of which pledge themselves not to indulge in wasteful practices of this kind. Today, when so much importance is attached by the makers of policy to economic development, the question whether a higher proportion of the farmer's income could not be ploughed back into the land is a matter of concern to many people.

It is true that the re-investment of farm incomes in farming too often takes the form of employing more labour to clear more ground, rather than of using new techniques to preserve the soil and improve the yield of existing farms, as most of the experts concerned with tropical farming would wish. It is true too that resources which might be used to raise the standard of living of their possessor, as some Europeans measure it, are diverted to ends which compete with this. When the choices made by tropical farmers become the subject of moral judgments, it is important to be quite clear what criteria are being used. On a wholly objective measurement of standards of living, the command of a larger total of goods to be consumed or enjoyed is a rise in standards however the total is made up. But if it is assumed that some particular good, such as health, *ought* to be given preference, then it will be argued that standards have not *really* risen, unless houses are more hygienic, food more nutritious, and so on; and that if resources that could have been used to achieve this have been used otherwise expenditure has been wasteful. Again, when it is argued that cash incomes are squandered instead of being used to increase productivity, it is sometimes forgotten that what may be unproductive expenditure in one society need not be so in another. Take the oft-quoted example of the ubiquitous bicycle: a bicycle in a country where public transport is inadequate can be invaluable as a means of transport for the small producer.

Expenditure on feasts cannot always be so readily justified in terms of economic advantage. Yet this does sometimes have a directly economic function. In a Malay fishing village feasts are not given only on such occasions as weddings. Men may give them when they like, and they do give them when they want to raise money for what can fairly be called capital investment, to buy a new net for example. How is this? Because at a Malay feast the guests bring gifts to the host, and it is now the established custom that the gifts are made in cash. Of course a host only expects to receive gifts from people to whom he has previously made similar gifts. But when all of these give him money at the same time, he can expect to receive an appreciable amount. The process is not unlike cashing one's savings, and as soon as one uses this phrase one sees that from the giver's point of view his action is analogous to saving. Of course it is not as economically efficient a method as putting the same amount in the bank; but then it also serves the social end of keeping on good terms with one's neighbours and showing that one is not beholden to them.

In Africa, by contrast, feasts are purely social events, and bring no such economic return. They are occasions for competitive display, as indeed are comparable occasions in Western society, and it is undeniable that most African farmers would allocate resources to feasting before they considered that re-investment of income which economists tell us is essential for healthy economic growth. Perhaps it should be added that this proposition of economics has not been expounded to them.

A Dutch anthropologist, A. J. K. Köbben, described two types of expenditure by rich cocoa farmers in the Ivory Coast.[1] Neither was actually a form of re-investment, but one earned the approval of local Europeans while the other did not. One man, who had held the office of chief (i.e. an executive official of the French administration) had a large house furnished in European style to which he invited Europeans when they came to his village. The others displayed their wealth by the lavish distribution of meat, drink, cigarettes and cash at funeral ceremonies. The first was held to be ranging himself on the side of the Europeans against his own people, and his wealth made him an object of envy and hatred; the others were admired for their ability to practise customary forms of generosity on a more than customary scale. Their expediture won the esteem of their fellows, the reward for conformity with expectations. Most reasonable men value this as much as they do health, intellectual pleasure or material comforts.

Of course there are many places where to have a house of European style is an admissible way of displaying one's wealth; it inspires envy, as every display of wealth is intended to do, but not rancour. But there are few if any places where people are expected to increase their own material possessions by

1. *Le Planteur Noir*, 1956

curtailing their generosity towards those who have a claim on it, whether by virtue of kinship or of favours given in the past. It is true in any society that rich men who are considered mean are not admired. But the values of Western society make accumulation easier by narrowing the field of persons whose claims on any individual are recognised. Men in newly industrialised societies who want to adopt Western values in this respect are almost constrained to leave the environment where they are surrounded by their kinsmen and friends, and strike out a new life elsewhere. This is the explanation of the so-called conservatism of rural areas in terms of the social structure, of what men have been taught to expect of their fellows, and not of the character of individuals. And it must be remembered that what is usually meant by conservatism in this context is not unwillingness to make *any* adjustment to new circumstances, but unwillingness to make all the adjustments which outsiders think, and sometimes even know, are desirable.

Land Rights

The conception of land as a source of indirect profit—of the control over land as a means of increasing one's material wealth by making others pay for the use of it—is necessarily absent in a non-commercial society. In such societies, where people meet nearly all their needs by directly exploiting the natural resources of their own environment, the right to land is a condition of existence, and the land of a group—whether a whole people or a subdivision of it—is commonly conceived as a patrimony to be jealously preserved, and is often the focus of religious beliefs and practices. Of course the intensity of attachment to particular fields must vary with the mode of life. There are still a few wholly nomadic herdsmen whose interest in land is limited to security of access to pastures, and rather more societies of cultivators whose practice is for a whole village to move every few years when its land is exhausted. But we may take as typical the peoples where there is continuity of settlement, and some at least of the population of each local community have succeeded their forefathers in occupation of its land. In such societies the right to land for cultivation is conceived almost as a right of citizenship. It is inherent in membership of a group with corporate rights, normally a group of kin. Most commonly in Africa and Oceania the rights of the group do not override the right of the individual farmer to the unrestricted occupation of his land, to cultivate as he pleases and to transmit it to his heirs. Occasionally all the members of a right-holding group may cultivate their lands together on a common plan. But the essential feature of this so-called 'communal' ownership of land is the control of the group over alienation—that is over the admission of non-members to the use of group land.

Wherever the area of land available is limited, whether because people live on islands or near powerful neighbours, or because there is pressure of population on the kind of land they like to live on, accepted arrangements exist for the admission of outsiders to land that is surplus to the needs of the right-holding group. For example the Kikuyu, who even before the coming of Europeans were fairly densely concentrated on their narrow ridges in the Kenya Highlands, had a quite elaborate set of names to describe 'strangers' established on group land, according to the nature of the arrangement made with them. There were two characteristic types of arrangement: the initiative might come from an outsider whose own group was short of land, or from a right-holder who had some urgent need, perhaps for an animal to pay a fine or make a sacrifice or a marriage payment, and borrowed this from a friend, offering him the use of a field as security. The latter was the more directly economic transaction, though it should be noted that the land so pledged might be redeemed at any time, however distant. In the former case what the right-holder expected to gain was not anything material. His 'tenant' was expected at harvest to bring him a present of grain, or of the beer which was brewed from it. But this was not conceived as a rent; it was an acknowledgment of dependence, a recognition that the 'stranger' was legally there on sufferance. It was the fact of having such a client under his protection that was valued, for this enhanced the status of the protector and added to the number of people who would support him in a lawsuit, or if necessary a fight, and could be called upon for small services. As time went on the client relationship would often be forgotten, and the descendants of the 'stranger' come to be regarded as members of the right-holding group. But this was the only way in which he could establish an unconditional right to his land.

The substitution of cash for the annual grain payment or the loan of the cow may make great changes in attitudes to rights in land and relationships based on such rights. Not only is there a new incentive to get as much as possible for the grant of rights, but in some areas there is competition to obtain rights. This applies particularly to the limited areas of land where profitable crops can be grown. It applies also to land on the outskirts of towns where people who have made money seek to build handsome houses.

The question now becomes acute whether it is right to maintain the old rule that land could never finally pass out of the hands of the original right-holders. The 'stranger' who acquires a cocoa farm offers a larger sum for it if it is understood that the land is passing finally to him; but the laws of Ghana and Nigeria still do not admit that it can do so. The same is true of land sites in the neighbourhood of towns such as Ibadan or Abeokuta, though these are openly advertised for sale. The colonial governments of West Africa were concerned for a long time lest African populations should improvidently sell or mortgage all their land and so find themselves landless while farming was still their only source of subsistence. This view has been opposed by arguments in favour of the recognition and formal record of transfer. But measures to this end were never taken, and the new West African governments do not seem to be contemplating anything of the kind at present.

In Eastern and Southern Africa there are some places where individual rights have been introduced by law, as was done earlier and on a much wider scale in India. To give to rights of a new kind the status of laws which a superior government will uphold is one way of offering new opportunities to people who are alive to the possibilities of advantage. The grant of private rights in land was seen in India as the way to a higher level of civilisation. An early Indian Civil Servant saw it as the action which would stand as the memorial of British rule when all its material constructions were lying in ruins.[1] In the cases where individual freehold was created in Africa, this was conceived as the surest way of protecting the rights of Africans against the encroachment of aliens; in the most conspicuous case, that of the African kingdom of Buganda, the missionary friends of the African chiefs advised them to ask for it. It is interesting to see what use has been made of the right of free disposal of land by the people on whom it has been conferred.

Naturally a good deal depends upon the place in the pre-existing structure of the people who have been made freehold owners. If freehold rights are conferred upon cultivators, they become able to encumber their land without consulting their kinsmen, as many have already done in places where the law does not allow them to. If rights are conferred upon the heads of right-holding groups such men become the landlords of the rest of the right-holders. In fact the people who have been made into landlords in this way have been political overlords, and the people who were previously liable to pay them taxes have become instead liable to pay them rent. The political aspect of this development is more appropriately considered in the context of changes in political structure.

As to the economic aspect—the way in which freehold rights are turned to advantage—a good deal depends upon the size of holding, and the fact about the freehold estates that have been granted in Africa is that they have been either much too large or much too small to be developed as cash crop farms by their owners. The estates allotted to the Ganda nobles averaged eight square miles in area, and they first turned their good fortune to account by selling off parts of them; indeed, most of them had to sell some land to pay the cost of survey. What were the motives of the buyers? It has been remarked that in an agrarian society land is the safest investment, and the African or Indian farmer who has a little money to spare is not offered the variety of investments that compete for small savings

---

1. W. W. Hunter, *Orissa*, 1872, vol. 2, p. 200, quoted by F. G. Bailey, *Caste and the Economic Frontier*, 1957, p. 242

in Western countries; moreover he is apt to regard the Post Office Savings Bank with some suspicion. It is also true that the owner of land is not dependent on a landlord. But to many Ganda this last statement is as significant in a social as in an economic sense. The Ganda were a socially stratified society in the sense that chiefs, those who exercised authority, were distinguished from peasants, those who were subject to authority. Today there are still chiefs who exercise authority in the formal political system, but landlords are assimilated to chiefs in the popular view, and indeed are expected to exercise some of the functions of chiefs in relation to their tenants. By becoming a landowner any man can attain the social status of chief, and by having even one tenant he can establish that relationship of patron to client which still confers prestige. The original landowners were not slow to translate the old claims of chiefs upon their subjects into cash exactions, but limits were early set by law upon this form of enterprise.

Very different consequences came from the introduction of freehold rights in the Union of South Africa. This happened in a village of refugees from the inter-tribal wars of the early nineteenth century, who sought protection in the Ciskeian area of the Cape Colony. A number of such refugee villages were formed at the time; they were considered to hold their land under the 'communal' tenure of native custom unless they asked for freehold allotments. In the Ciskei there is no profitable export crop, and indeed the farm holdings are too small to produce more than a bare subsistence which is supplemented by work for wages in the cities. So the essential advantage conferred by freehold tenure is freedom from interference in the transmission of land. In the villages where the tenure is that of native custom the headman has the right to re-allot vacant fields. His action has to be confirmed by a Native Commissioner, and in fact it has come to be the Native Commissioner who makes the decisions. Regulations define the circumstances in which a holding is deemed to be abandoned, in a way which limits the customary right of an absentee to come back after any length of time and claim his land. If it is abandoned, or the holder dies without near kin, the Native Commissioner's choice for a successor is the man who has waited longest in the village. But there are often others who have a better right in terms of kinship. In the freehold area no one can lose his land against his will, and men can go away to the towns, taking their wives with them, and leave the farm with a relative, or lease it, as they please. Here land, scarce as it is, has no commercial value: it cannot be turned to profitable account and would neither be offered not accepted as security for a debt. So that the effect of the grant of freehold rights has been to enable the land-owners to resist further inroads upon the customary system.

China and India have not had to wait for Western influences to develop commercial transactions in land. In China the rich south-eastern provinces, for example, had long had their land-lords and tenants, their debtors and creditors, and their land-less labourers. The landlords indeed were the main source of rural credit, and so the persons of greatest influence in the village and its spokesmen in dealings with the world outside; Fei Hsiao-tung has called this class 'the gentry'. Here the significant effect of the entry of China into world trade was the growth of a new merchant class who were able to build up wealth on a scale previously unknown, and to invest part of it in land which they regarded purely as a source of income, being themselves strangers to the village. In the interior the same process took place, though perhaps on a smaller scale, as com-munications improved and trade over larger areas became practicable. Yet, right up to the introduction of the Communist régime, land was still regarded as being in principle the patri-mony of future generations, and was sold only when the owners had no other way to meet their obligations, often those imposed by ritual requirements such as marriage and funeral ceremonies. The principle that a man's land should be divided among his sons was also maintained, and before the era of large-scale commerce the periodical redistribution which this involved prevented the accumulation of very large areas in a few people's hands. But it is a corollary of this principle that there must be additional resources available for people whose holdings are too small to yield them subsistence. In Africa the solution was found either in clearing virgin bush or in the non-monetary transactions which have been described. In China it was found to a large extent in the development of village crafts to supplement the resources of the land. But another effect of the importation of machine-made goods has been to displace the hand-made village products, or to make them dependent on oversea trade, as in the case of the substitution of imported for locally spun cotton thread.

An example from India, of a hill village in Orissa, shows the effects of a century of external political and economic influence on a village which was largely self-subsistent, or else dependent on the barter of rice, up to the time when it was annexed to British India.[1] Here the British authorities formally recognised private property in land, and so placed it beyond doubt that they would regard sales of land as legal transactions, but one may question whether this legal act had any consequences that would not have been produced eventually by economic pressures. Again we see land passing out of the hands of cultivators into those of people with other sources of income, in this case the descendants of the immigrants who came to the village when in 1855, immediately after the annexation of the district, it was made the headquarters of an administrative division. Some of these immigrants were paid servants of the government, others were traders who came in to supply the needs of the paid employees. Most of them came from neighbouring agricultural communities which had been introduced to the commercial economy a little earlier. The traders in particular intended to remain there permanently, and so sought to become landowners; they too found land the best investment for their profits.

Why should the villagers sell their land? The reason suggested is that the new commercial influences stimulated the earlier division of family lands. The traditional principle of the Indian joint family is that as long as a man lives his sons are under his authority and all the economic resources of the family are pooled. As the villagers themselves found sources of income outside farming, they became unwilling to pool them, and it became usual for the family land to be divided as soon as all

1. See F. G. Bailey, *Caste and the Economic Frontier*, 1957

55

the brothers were married and could set up their own households. This only hastened a division which was bound to be made eventually, but it is argued that the process has reduced the size of farms to a point where their yield gives no surplus for contingencies, whether the loss of a plough or the obligation to perform a ceremony, so that most people can only meet an emergency by selling land.

The study of cocoa farmers in Ghana which has already been quoted illustrates some of the new relationships that may be established when the attraction of a profitable cash crop draws immigrants to a particular type of land. Most commonly such immigrants are single individuals, but one Ghanaian practice has been for a number of men from the same neighbourhood—not necessarily kinsmen—jointly to offer a sum of money for a fairly large area which they then divide into strips and farm independently. This has the effect of keeping the land of village neighbours together, but it is not clear from the published information whether that is the reason for operating in 'companies', as these groups are called. When new cocoa land has been acquired the next step is to bring it under cultivation, work which involves cutting down the tall trees of the rain-forest. It was rare for the farmers who had originally acquired the land to clear and plant it by themselves. More commonly they employed labourers, who might be rewarded, when the crop came into bearing, by a two-third share of the cocoa harvested or else by being given a share of the land. The share-cropping arrangement is found among all the Akan-speaking peoples, but not with Nigerian cocoa-farmers, and it seems to have its origin in the claim of the chiefs to one-third of 'whatever came out of the land' (gold, wild rubber, etc). The employer often takes two-thirds of the cocoa harvested by his labourers, but the division into three seems to have its roots firmly fixed in tradition. It is worth noting that in those areas where land was already scarce at the time when cocoa was introduced, opinion was opposed to the grant of rights to strangers, and the practice never grew up of rewarding labourers by transferring land rights.

Sources of Credit

As cash transactions replace barter, traders need capital before they can begin operations. In West Africa the organisation that has developed to meet this need is the contribution club, the counterpart of which has long been established in China. In Africa the members of these clubs are generally people who have not enough education to qualify them for salaried posts and so have no regular income out of which they can save. In some parts of the Ibo country in Eastern Nigeria the staple foods have to be imported even in the rural areas. There is no organisation for export from the districts which have a surplus; traders from the shortage areas go to buy there. The initial outlay may be small, but it is indispensable, and it is obtained by joining a contribution club. These clubs have regular meetings at each of which a member pays in an agreed share, and the whole amount is handed over there and then to one member; each in turn is entitled to the 'take-out'. The members whose turn comes early in the cycle thus draw out a good deal more than they have put in, but they are of course expected to keep up their membership until they have paid their full share, and at the time when a member receives the 'take-out' he has to produce a signed guarantee to this effect from a senior kinsman. Naturally there is a good deal of competition for the early 'take-outs', since the order is not settled by chance but by one of the officials of the club, who is usually open to arguments reinforced by gifts; it is said that these are sometimes made on a scale that considerably reduces the value of the 'take-out'. Nevertheless, this provides a means of meeting unforeseen contingencies as well as of starting in trade; the confidence of the members in one another comes from personal knowledge backed up by the guarantee of kinsmen, and people can get credit in this way when no impersonal agency would give it them. The Chinese societies, as would be expected of a people well used to calculating rates of interest, had more elaborate rules, each member's payment being related to the length of time he must wait before taking the 'pool', and as large-scale trade developed this kind of credit system came to be operated on an impressive scale.

CHAPTER 3

NEW FAMILIES

Types of kin group—The homestead of the Tallensi—Wider significance of the lineage—Chinese lineages—Lineage and marriage—Marriage payments—Contrasts with Western values—Marriage in matrilineal societies—Marriage in changing Africa—Legal marriage as a status symbol—Marriage in Singapore—Change in matrilineal societies.

WHEN PEOPLE discuss changes in family organisation, whether in the Western world or in more recently industrialised countries, they often deplore the fact that the family has lost many of the functions that it used to have. It would be truer to say that the social group which used to be thought of as the family has become smaller, and that the family of today cannot possibly do for its members what some earlier types of family did. Obviously a good deal of confusion must be caused if people use 'family' indiscriminately to mean a couple with their children, a polygamous household, or all a person's traceable kin, and social anthropologists have taken some pains to sort out and distinguish these and other different kinds of kin groups. It is possible in any society to identify the 'elementary' or 'nuclear' family of parents with their children. But in small-scale societies the members of the elementary family go through life in close contact with the parents' kin, and look to them for co-operation in many of the matters in which the family (in this sense) is not self-sufficient, whereas in urban, industrialised populations such co-operation is sought in relationships to which kinship is irrelevant.

In a society based on status, to use Maine's phrase, a significant part of a person's social relationships is defined by his membership, not of a class, the category which Westerners think of when discussing status, but of a family and a descent group to which the family is linked by one or other parent.

This is due largely to the simple fact that in circumstances where travel is difficult or dangerous, people usually spend their lives in the place where they were born or somewhere near it. The ideal of family unity, which exists in one form or another in every society, in these conditions dictates that close relations should live close together, and in the pre-literate societies of Africa and Oceania small villages will be found to consist wholly of kinsmen, and larger villages will have separate sections inhabited by close kin. Many of the villages of Europe, too, are still clusters of kin.

Types of Kin Group

It can be taken for granted, then, that in small-scale societies any body of people living in close concentration will be linked by kin ties of some kind. Frequently kinsmen linked by descent form a property-holding or co-operating group, but this is not always so. A conspicuous exception is the 'long-house' of the interior of Borneo.[1] Here what would elsewhere be the population of a whole village live in a single building 100 yards long or even more. The long-house stands on piles beside one of the rivers that are the only means of communication. It is divided into separate compartments, and it can be extended at any time by building on at the end. Each apartment is the home of an independent family. The inhabitants of every apartment are there because one of them is a kinsman of some-one who was living in the long-house when he came there. But there is no rule that obliges anyone to live in any particular long-house; on the other hand claims to a share in family property, such as rice-fields, cannot be established in any way except by living in the house. People usually decide where they will live at the time when they marry, and they can attach themselves to any kinsman of husband or wife. Naturally one thing that they consider when they make their choice is their chance of getting rice-land. In such a system people's freedom

1. *See* J. D. Freeman, 'The Family System of the Iban of Borneo' in J. R. Goody, ed., *The Developmental Cycle in Domestic Groups*, 1958.

of choice is limited by the range of kinship ties—nobody could join a long-house where he had no kin—but the elementary family is not closely bound to any one set of kinsmen.

But more commonly the family is permanently tied to the wider body of kin that anthropologists call a *descent group* or *lineage*. A *lineage* consists of persons related by descent through *one* of their two parents; if descent is traced through the father it is *patrilineal*, if through the mother, *matrilineal*. Lineage membership carries with it rights to property—land, cattle, a boat, a share in a business, or whatever—and lineage kin are expected to support one another in securing redress for wrongs. Lineages are usually *exogamous*; that is, members of the same lineage may not marry. In a patrilineal system every person has definite rights and duties which fall to him in virtue of his own lineage membership and of his ties with other lineages, those of his mother, his wife, and the men who marry his sisters and daughters. These relationships fill the greater part of his total social field.

The fact that most small-scale societies permit polygamy is probably better known than anything else about them. But it is of very much less significance than the kinship principles just described. The polygynous family, in which the head of the household has more than one wife, has been described as a number of elementary families linked by a common father. The number is rarely more than two, and many men in polygynous societies have only one wife.

Lineages do not usually proliferate through the generations; as the ties of common ancestry grow more remote, what was one property-holding group splits into two or more. The significant group for purposes of everyday life is sometimes called the *nuclear* lineage, and this is seldom wider than the children of a common grandfather. This group is also sometimes called the *extended family,* and when this term is used the spouses of the lineage members, who themselves come from other lineages, are included.

The most closely knit form of extended family is the Indian *joint family*, which shares a single dwelling, its component families having their separate rooms around a courtyard, and also holds property in common; the fields are tilled jointly by all the men of the group, the food that is harvested is kept in a common store and cooked jointly by the women to provide a common meal for the whole group, and income earned from the sale of group produce is pooled and administered by the family head. The members join in religious rites which are performed by the family head on their behalf. The basis for the development of such a family is the rule that a man is subject to his father's authority as long as his father is alive, and should live under his roof. So a joint family is built up as sons marry and bring their wives home. The size which it reaches depends upon the life-span of the father. When he dies the brothers generally separate; if he has lived a very long time the new families which are now founded will themselves contain married sons.

Nowhere else do we find this complete community of living and community of property, but the ideal of the lasting unity of the descendants of one father, of common residence, and of the recognition of the senior man's authority, is found in all patrilineal societies. The classical literature of China, as well as that of India, insists upon this ideal, although there is evidence that for large numbers of the population it was never more than an ideal; and the traditions of the Japanese family, which are still pointed to by conservative Japanese as embodying a morality superior to that of the present day, are similar, except that in Japan it was only the eldest son who was expected to live all his life under his father's roof.

The Homestead of the Tallensi

The actual organisation and lay-out of such compound households in a number of African societies have been described at first hand. One of the most detailed accounts is that given by Fortes[1] of the Tallensi, a population of subsistence farmers and cattle owners in the interior of Ghana. At the time when Fortes lived among them, the Tallensi maintained a system of social relationships which, as it seemed to them, had persisted unchanged from the remote past.

1. M. Fortes, *The Web of Kinship among the Tallensi*, 1949

A homestead among the Tallensi is a cluster of mud huts, linked by an encircling wall and entered by a narrow gateway which can be closed at night. Inside is a room in which the head of the household maintains the shrines of his ancestors, and a series of rooms (each a separate hut) for his wives and the wives of his sons; in each of these lives a wife with her young children. There may also be a widowed mother. If necessary, there will be a room for adolescent boys to sleep in. Attached to each wife's living-room is a store room and a kitchen, but a common granary stands in the middle of the enclosure, and there is a single grinding-room to which the women come in turn to grind the grain that is handed out to them by the household head. Only he may take grain from the granary, but it is his duty to distribute it absolutely equally between the component families; that is to say, each wife has the same share regardless of the number of her children. Each wife normally cooks for her own family, though she may send portions to others in times of plenty. When grain is scarce the wives may cook in turn for the whole household. The men work together on the land of the group.

The head of the household must see that all its members are supplied from its joint resources with the necessities of daily life. He must also arrange for such outlay as may need to be made on their account for other purposes. Most important among these is the marriage of the young men as they come to the appropriate age. As in many other pre-literate societies, a marriage is made legal by the transfer of goods from the husband to the kin of the wife, a subject which will have to be discussed later; with the Tallensi the goods consist in fowls and cattle, creatures which are not used for everyday food but only for sacrificial meals. There are regular occasions when sacrifices have to be made, and in addition, if a member of the household falls ill a diviner—who receives a fee in kind—may indicate that a special sacrifice must be offered to the spirit which has caused the sickness. Also, a member may be guilty of a misdemeanour for which compensation has to be paid. It is the responsibility of the head of the household to deal with all these contingencies.

Nevertheless, individuals are allowed to acquire property which is their own. Every family has its own fowls, and little boys are quite early given one or two of these to breed from. Men can acquire sheep and goats—though not cattle—which are recognised to be their own property, though the head of the household can make use of them or can refuse to allow the owner to do so. Some property comes into the group from outside—from relatives of the women who have married into it, the uncles and grandfathers of their children. Some is acquired by trading; a woman who gets extra grain in either of these ways is entitled to keep it to feed her own children. Also there is a rule that the cattle received at the marriage of a girl should be used for the marriage of her full brother if she has one of marriageable age.

The ideal father, here as everywhere, is wise and just. If he uses his son's stock, either it should be for his son's benefit—for example as part of his marriage payment—or he should make a return for it by some outlay from the common pool later on. If a son feels that he is not being treated fairly, he will leave the group and set up his own household; yet he cannot do this unless the head agrees. But often this division does not take place as long as the head of the household is alive. Sometimes one member of the group will decide to farm independently without leaving the common household. Then the fields will be divided, and within the family enclosure a wall will be built around his section, and he will make his own entrance-gate.

These examples show how the elementary family, without losing its identity, can for the greater part of its existence be a unit in a larger whole. It depends on the pooled resources of this wider household for a large proportion of its daily needs, and also for any special outlay that it may require. While its members are young adults, and often even longer, they are subject to the authority of a senior man who is their religious as well as their secular head. This authority is, in essence, parental authority; it is an extension of parental authority beyond the span which modern Western society considers appropriate to it. But within the component families of such a household, every father has the same authority and the same responsibility for his own children.

Something has been said about what women can do by their outside activities to increase the supply of food for their own children. The tie between a mother and her own children is equally strong all over the world, but in the household composed of linked families the social environment of the young child is wider than it is in the isolated families of Western cities. Women can turn at need to the other women of the household; they help one another over difficult times such as pregnancy and childbirth. An older woman can look after young children while their own mother is away at the market, or on one of the long arduous journeys to collect firewood. Children are part of a group of contemporaries from the time when they can walk. At the low standard of expectations of the Tallensi, the resources needed to meet most circumstances of special strain are available within the walls of the homestead.

There are both advantages and disadvantages in belonging to such a group, as there are in belonging to any close-knit group. At times the advantages of the common pool of labour and material resources seem to be outweighed by the disadvantages of subordination to the common head. Such dissatisfaction may arise from a clash of temperaments, but it is commonly expressed, and felt to be justified, in conflicts over the allocation of resources. Fortes[1] quotes a Tallensi proverb that households break up 'because of hens and eggs'; that is to say, when someone considers that the head of the household has been unreasonable in the exercise of his over-riding control over the members' property. In descriptions of pastoral peoples in both eastern and western Africa we read how it is every man's ambition to have independent control of his share of the family herd. Here we see already in existence the disruptive forces which modern economic conditions, reinforced by Western conceptions of family life, have strengthened.

1. *Op. cit.*, p. 207

Wider Significance of the Lineage

Lineage membership can have considerable political significance. Often members of particular lineages have higher rank than others; this is most marked in societies that have hereditary rulers. At the other end of the political scale, where there are no judicial institutions, or where chiefs and elders hold courts but do not command any organisation comparable to a police force to execute their decisions, people rely on their kinsmen to secure redress for their wrongs. For example, among the Nuer of the southern Sudan, whose traditional system has been described as one of 'ordered anarchy', if a man was killed it was the duty of his kinsmen to seek revenge by instituting a feud against the killer, or if cattle were stolen the owner would go with the support of his kinsmen to get them back. There have been many societies where, though people were not expected to take the law into their own hands without reference to some authority, after the case had been heard the injured party was entitled to seize the compensation adjudged to be his due; for such forceful action, again, he relied on his kinsmen. Frequently the lineage has been treated by superior authorities as a political unit, the head being responsible for the conduct of all its members, and sometimes for the performance of obligations such as the payment of tax, or even army service, as in the African kingdom of Ruanda.

Very commonly the lineage is a religious unit, and its head has the duty of performing the necessary rites to obtain from the ancestors the benefits and protection that they are believed to confer. In African societies an aspect of this ritual leadership is responsibility for consulting a diviner when a lineage member falls sick (since this is always held to be due to the action of some supernatural being) and making the sacrifice which the divination shows to be called for.

As has been illustrated in the description of the Tallensi, the lineage is a property-owning unit. Every lineage member has a right to a share in its property. If the property consists in stock, it is redistributed when the senior man dies. If it is land, a member can assert his right to a share as soon as he sets up house. On the other hand, he is not obliged to live on his lineage land; he can live on that of his mother's or even his wife's lineage if he likes, but his children cannot acquire rights there. There rules contrast with those of *non-unilineal* societies such as the dwellers in the Borneo long-houses. There too a man can live where he likes, but his only claim on land is derived from his membership of a long-house, and he could not inherit from his father unless he was living in the same long-house when his father died.

In non-literate societies the number of generations through which common descent is traced is not usually large; in technical terms, the *maximal lineage* is not of *wide span*. It is of the essence of the lineage that genealogical relationships can actually be traced; claims and obligations must rest, as they do in Western societies, on something more than a common name. Links are traced further for some purposes than for others; the property-owning unit may consist of the descendants of a common grandfather while the ritual unit looks back one or two generations further.

Descent groups of this kind in subsistence societies have usually lost their cohesion on the introduction of a money economy. The previous chapter described the break-up of farms in an Indian village as members of the farming family began to earn cash incomes independently of their brothers, became unwilling to pool their incomes and insisted on the division of the family property. It has been argued that corporate property-owning groups based on descent cannot survive in a society which allows of great inequality in individual incomes; the richer members will never consent to a system of joint administration by the senior man.

Chinese Lineages

What seems at first sight a striking exception to this generalisation comes from the south-eastern provinces of China, Fukien and Kwantung.[1] Here there are, or were up to the Communist revolution, villages of up to three thousand people inhabited by members of a single lineage which traces its common genealogy seven hundred years back. The first thing

1. M. Freedman, *Lineage Organisation in South-eastern China*, 1958

worth noting about these cohesive lineages is that the members did not share equally, as of right, in the land; it was allocated on quite different principles. This system exists alongside the typical system whereby the land of a simple or polygynous family is distributed among the sons on the death of the father. For most Chinese, the result of this more common system was that if the portions were too small somebody had to emigrate, or rent land from a landlord, or find some other source of livelihood; the corresponding solutions in Africa would be to open up new land (perhaps only a few hundred yards away), or make some kind of arrangement with a right-holder of another lineage, or, in modern times, go away and work for wages.

But in these large Chinese lineage-villages, all, or nearly all, the villagers were living on lineage land. This was possible because at some time in the past areas of land had been set aside for common lineage purposes; not for common cultivation, but for their produce to be devoted to lineage interests. The most important of these were religious. The returns from lineage land went to keep up the halls in which ancestor tablets were kept, and to meet the cost of the rites performed there at regular intervals. Another common purpose which was met from the same resources was the education of members of the lineage to pass the examinations by which people entered the Chinese bureaucracy; the fields set aside for this purpose were known as 'book-lamp-lands'.

Sometimes these lands were cultivated in turn by the different sections of the lineage, and the cultivators at any given time were responsible for the religious expenses of the lineage as a whole; under such an arrangement, every so often a few people had a little more land than usual to cultivate. The other arrangement was that the leading men of the lineage—*not* the seniors in line of descent, but the most prominent, which is apt to mean the richest—managed the common land on a business basis, letting it for the best rent they could get. Members of the lineage had priority over other people in getting tenancies, but they got no easier terms. All the same, the great majority of the tenants of lineage land were lineage members. In the depression years between the two world wars, Chinese writers of radical views saw as much exploitation of the tenant in this system as in any other form of landlordism. The lineage funds for education seem also to have gone more often to the sons of distinguished families than to bright boys from obscure ones.

Yet the lineage held together. The poorer members preferred to live in the same place and be exploited by their own lineage kin rather than by some other landlord. Why? Dr Freedman suggests that the mere existence of a lineage fund of wealth, from which they might perhaps hope some day for a bigger share, was one influence. Another was the prestige which the whole lineage got from its élite—its rich and educated men. Moreover, these men had power as well as prestige; in dealing with the outside world, and particularly with the government, they were in a position to help their lineage kin, whereas a man in a poor lineage had nobody he could look to, even theoretically, for help.

The very forces which have broken up lineage solidarity elsewhere are the ones that reinforced it in south-eastern China. Perhaps the reason is that in this region, where land is unusually productive, profits were to be made by trading the surplus of the same crop that was grown for subsistence. Whereas in many other countries the road to riches has led away from the ancestral land, here the land itself was a source of profit and the profits were invested in more land; and later, as the opening-up of China to world trade created new sources of profit for middlemen, these profits too were invested in land. But why was this treated as lineage and indivisible, and not as family and divisible, property? One answer is in the function of the property as a religious endowment. The founding of a new ancestral hall, at the moment when it was done, marked the claim of one branch of a lineage to high status—the status attained by being able to afford your own ancestral hall and celebrate your own rites. At that point in time it *was* an assertion of the separate identity of one section of the larger lineage. But this was the reverse of the more common process of the division of lineage property so that a new section can become autonomous; it brought property in instead of taking it out.

Lineage and Marriage

Where the family is linked with a continuing lineage, the attitude towards progeny is different from what it is in contemporary Western society. People do not wish to have children only for the sake of the delight that they expect to take in them, although in most non-commercial societies this feeling is clearly shown in behaviour and often expressed in words. From the point of view of the lineage, it is a duty to have children; from the point of view of the individual father, he cannot look forward to establishing an independent household until he has sons old enough to help him in farming and herding; where the lineage is the members' defence against encroachments on their rights, it is important that it should be strong in numbers. Where it controls a joint patrimony, there is always a strong feeling that this property should not go to 'strangers' for lack of direct heirs—a reflection of the sense of solidarity within the lineage, the sense that its members are closer to one another than to anyone outside.

Everywhere except in Muslim countries, it is through their descendants that people attain immortality in a more specific sense than Rupert Brooke's; their memory and, as they see it, their life in the spirit world are maintained by the sacrifices to them that only their direct descendants can make, and in popular Chinese belief the dead who have no descendants to care for them are thought to haunt the living. The Hindu religion makes it a duty to beget a son who will perform the family rites.

Thus the desire to be sure of progeny is one of the strongest reasons why polygynous marriages are permitted and contracted, though the more mundane reasons for seeking to build up a large household naturally also play their part. This is true particularly of societies living at subsistence level where the pressure of population is not very great, so that a large farming group can extend its cultivation as widely as its resources allow. In commercial societies too, a large household can deploy manpower in ways that are not practicable for a small one, such as dividing time between farm work and other gainful activities.

People depend, then, on their kinsmen in various circumstances for which Western societies provide in other ways. In Western societies one earns a living by entering into some contract of employment. Family connections may be helpful in this, but they do not confer any rights, and the ideal character is the one who makes his own way without those advantages of birth that have come to be regarded as adventitious.

Rather paradoxically, many of the people in the Western world who attach most importance to the sanctity of family life do not realise that lineage systems are based on that very conception—on the idea that the tie which binds children to parents has priority over all others. This is the ideal of the family in the traditions of India, China and Japan, all of which hold that in case of any conflict of interests the claim of filial duty must come first without question. It must be emphasised that this *is* an ideal, which is buttressed by religion, and can be supported by appeals to moral sentiments of just the same kind as are invoked by Christians on behalf of the elementary family of spouses with their children. The difference between the two ideals lies in the place which they give to the tie between husband and wife. In Christian theory this is the bond which should be indissoluble and should have absolute priority, and members of Western society who do not adhere to the Christian religion, though many of them do not subscribe to the principle of indissoluble marriage, would also regard it as impermissible for relatives of the spouses to have authority to break a marriage up. Still less does Western society regard it as tolerable that the choice of marriage partners should be dictated by parents or relatives; though there may be, even today, more room for parental pressure than is generally admitted.

The situation in which the kinsmen of the spouses have a formally recognised interest in the making, maintenance and breaking of a marriage is commonly described by the cliché that 'marriage is an affair of groups and not of individuals'. This statement, which in a certain sense is true, is assumed to be derogatory, and this assumption is based on the further assumption that such a situation imposes hardships on women.

The standard case to which judgments of this kind refer

is that of a society where descent is traced in the male line, where the significant kin group is that of the sons and grandsons of one man, and where women are disposed of by their male relatives in such a way as to form advantageous alliances. These are the characteristics of traditional Chinese, Japanese and Indian societies and of many in Africa. But before the champions of oppressed femininity reach for their guns, they should remember that there are also societies where descent is traced in the female line, and there it is the husband who is in a precarious position and can be sent away by his wife's kin if they or she are not satisfied with him. Moreover, whereas Chinese and Japanese writings acknowledge that a man who is called upon to put away his wife in the interests of his kin group may be torn between affection and duty, we do not hear of such emotional conflicts in African matrilineal societies; the impression given by the records of anthropologists who have lived among them is that when a husband is dismissed it is usually with his wife's consent. Nevertheless, it must be admitted that in matrilineal as in patrilineal societies, the male guardian of a woman has always been regarded as formally entitled to dispose of her in marriage, and this sometimes makes it necessary for women to accept husbands who are distasteful to them.

Why should this be so? The commonly accepted interpretations in terms of inferior moral values are really not adequate. The ideal of family unity is held and expressed in every human society, and it is more directly supported by religion in those societies which practise the worship of ancestors than in those which do not. As has been remarked, the significant point here is that the group within which unity is held to be important is both wider than the elementary family and in some circumstances opposed to it. It is true that the romantic ideal of chivalry towards women is absent, as is the more modern ideal, which itself rejects the romantic one, of the equality of women with men.

Marriage Payments

In a patrilineal society marriage is something more than the arrangement by which a man founds his home and family. It is also his way of continuing the legitimate line, and is therefore of importance to the lineage as a body. This explains some features of African marriage procedure and law which have often been misunderstood, and sometimes even forbidden by missions or governments.

The best known characteristic of African marriage law is what was called, in the early days of South Africa, the sin of buying wives. In terms that are less question-begging, this is the rule that a marriage is made legal by the transfer of goods from the lineage kin of the bridegroom to those of the bride. This rule is not in itself peculiar to Africa. In non-literate societies every contract is attested and ratified by a transfer of goods, and every marriage is accompanied by the formal transfer of prescribed goods. These may be of different kinds and pass in different directions. Sometimes the purpose of the transfer is to provide initial resources for the new household, or to ensure that the wife will have support if her husband dies, as in dowry systems where the wife brings wealth with her. In a very small way some African families do equip their daughters with the elementary domestic outfit that their culture provides. But in Africa the transfer which gives legal recognition to a marriage always goes from the husband's side, and it is most substantial, and most important, in patrilineal societies where the children of the marriage will belong to the line of the husband.

There is here an idea of the equivalence between the cattle given by the husband's lineage and the children that the wife will bear. The children of a woman for whom no cattle have been given cannot be claimed as his by their father. On the other hand, the children of a woman for whom cattle have been given are counted as those of the man on whose behalf the cattle were given, whoever actually begot them. Finally, if a marriage is dissolved the cattle must be returned, but it is often the rule that if the woman has borne children the full number are not claimed. The fundamental principle is that stated by the Gusii of Kenya, that when the 'house is set up', and it can reasonably be expected, even where mortality is as high as it is in Africa, that the father's line will not die out, she has 'paid for herself'. All these principles have been summed up in the statement that what used to be called 'bride-price' is really 'child-price'.

Other consequences of this principle are unfamiliar, and have appeared repugnant to people who take one or other Western system of marriage laws and procedures for granted. A legal marriage in a patrilineal society makes the woman's children the legal progeny of her husband's lineage. The marriage is in being as long as the cattle which made it are in the possession of the woman's lineage; hence death does not dissolve the marriage unless the cattle are returned. A widow is not free to re-marry without this formal divorce procedure, and if she bears more children they are legally the children of her dead husband. She passes under the guardianship of her husband's heir, though she may not be required to cohabit with him sexually; she is expected to live in his homestead, and this is one way in which polygynous households are constituted.

But even when it is recognised that the transfer of cattle at a marriage is not the purchase of a woman, one may still ask why children have to be 'bought'. The answer might be that in a system of patrilineal descent, every lineage loses the children of its own women, who belong to the lines of their fathers; if a woman bears a child before marriage it remains with her father's lineage unless its father establishes a claim to it by a payment in cattle, which is less than the marriage payment. So the marriage cattle have been described as 'payment for the woman's fertility' or as a 'compensation for the loss of her fertility'. One might look at the question from the point of view of the husband's kin and say that, in giving him a wife, the woman's kin have done him the most valuable service possible; they have given him the means to continue his line, and if any service deserves a return gift it is this. This kind of interpretation would be borne out by the behaviour of peoples such as the Nyoro of Uganda, where a man all through his life must behave to his wife's kinsmen as an inferior does to someone from whom he has received a favour.

Interpretations of the marriage payment in such abstract terms are, of course, the work of the anthropologist and not of the people who marry by these procedures. The theory that it is in essence the woman's fertility which is transferred, and for which a return is made, is most strikingly borne out in those rare cases where a man who seeks a wife must give to her kinsmen not goods, but a woman of his own group. In such a system the woman's freedom of choice is severely restricted, since even if some marriages are freely agreed upon they have to be balanced by others in which this is not likely to be possible, and it is often necessary for girls to be committed in infancy so that obligations can be met. Therefore, 'marriage by exchange' has been forbidden by most European governments. But it is still remembered among such peoples as the Tiv of the Northern Region of Nigeria. Here children were not reckoned against cattle but against the children borne by the woman for whom a given wife was exchanged. There is a case on record where a woman wished to leave her husband, and it was held that since she had borne four children, the same number as her counterpart, she was free to do so.

There are certainly also ideas that people deserve gratitude for having brought up, and sometimes even for having begotten and borne, the girl who is being given as a wife. Among the Nuer, for example, if a girl's actual father is a man other than her mother's husband, he is entitled to a cow from among those received by the latter, known as 'the cow of the begetting', and if he has brought the bride up, he should receive additional beasts. Another example is that of the Plateau Tonga in Northern Rhodesia, where the midwife who delivered a girl—who is probably a kinswoman of her mother—receives a present at her marriage. Sometimes, too, the parents' grief at parting with their daughter is expressly recognised, as it is among the Nyoro, where the bridegroom's friends, when they go to fetch the bride, take with them a present of beer called 'that which comforts'; or among the Ashanti, where the girl's mother receives a special present of money (formerly meat) called the 'consolation fee'.

It would be a mistake, however, to imagine that the payment which acquires rights to a woman's children is necessarily accompanied by the transfer of her person. So far from the woman being herself bought and handed over to her husband, it is often the rule that she lives at her parents' home till her first child is born and reared, or, if she does live with her husband from the time when the marriage is formally concluded, she goes home for the birth of her children. The significance of this is in the maintenance of her ties with her own parents and other close kin.

In subsistence societies men rarely go to a great distance for their wives—indeed it is usually hard to travel great distances. So wives constantly visit their own homes, and when they do so they expect to be given presents of food (generally grain) to take home; it has been mentioned that this is one of the ways in which women among the Tallensi can acquire property which is under their own control. A woman's kinsmen maintain an interest in her children, even though they belong to another lineage. Where the wife lives at her own home till her first child is born, this child is sometimes left with its grandparents when she goes to her husband; and it is a very general rule that, although a child derives its legal rights from its father's line, it should be treated as a privileged person, entitled to special favour, at the home of its mother. In practice this rule is more important for adults than it is for children; it provides another direction in which anyone in difficulty can look for help. The ties of familiarity and affection are built up by much visiting of children at the homes of their kinsmen on both sides, for which there need not usually be any particular reason; though some people rationalise it, as do the Ganda, who maintain that a child is likely to be better brought up in the house of a relative than in that of its own parents. It was customary among the Ngoni in the days of their greatness for all children to be brought up by their grandparents. These, then, are the ways in which the elementary family is linked with wider groups.

The marriage payment, then, legalises a marriage, determines the legal paternity of children and creates the relationship of affinity between the kin of the spouses. The possession of the marriage cattle, which are distributed by the wife's father to his closest lineage kin, sometimes according to very strict rules, is the earnest of this relationship. It binds them on the one hand to an interest in the maintenance of the marriage, not only for the material reason that the cattle must be returned if it is dissolved, and on the other hand it gives them a special responsibility for the welfare of their kinswoman on whose behalf they have received the beasts.

Husbands do not often turn their wives out; it is the strength of a woman's position that her husband is more dependent upon her for the comforts of daily life than she is on him. More commonly, if there is a quarrel, the wife goes home and waits there for her husband to fetch her. It is the duty of those who hold the marriage cattle to know what has become of a runaway wife, and to return her to her husband, but not without requiring of him the appropriate amends if they are sure that he has been at fault.

These considerations may make it easier to understand why the cattle transfer, or in more recent times the transfer of a cash equivalent, has been found to be so indispensable in African eyes that the bans imposed on it have everywhere had to be lifted, and also that the reason is not the determination of African fathers to use their daughters as a source of gain. Yet one must still ask why they seek to impose their own wishes in the choice of their daughters' husbands, and how far mercenary calculations influence them.

It should be made clear that it is not the payment of cattle at marriage which creates for a woman the status of a perpetual minor. This is the status of women in all pre-industrial societies, and they begin to resent it as soon as they see the possibility of rejecting it. But the rejection more commonly takes the form of rejecting marriage altogether than of protesting against the marriage payment.

What then should be the interpretation of the paternal attitude? It is far too crude to see the father as a trader in women. One may grant that a father may hope to marry his daughters to men who will actually hand over the full number of cattle and not, as so often happens, leave half of them to be paid at some unspecified time in the future. One may grant that among peoples for whom cattle are the most highly valued

76

goods, a bride's lineage are keenly interested in the number and quality of those they are to receive, and sometimes insist on seeing them beforehand and rejecting those they consider to be of poor quality. One may grant that they enjoy the possession of the cattle, though it often happens that they enjoy this for only a short time, since they must use them as soon as they can to make another marriage.

But this is not the primary concern in the disposal of girls in marriage. The interests which are thought most important are of a kind that would have been taken for granted anywhere in Western Europe not so long ago.

It has been mentioned that in societies, such as the Nuer, which have no judical institutions people rely on their kinsmen for the protection of their most elementary rights. Even where political control is more highly developed, those who can muster a strong body of kinsmen often stand a better chance of getting their rights than those who cannot. This is a matter of mere numbers. In the economic field it is desirable that one's kin should be not only numerous but wealthy; then they will be able to assist in meeting those obligations—the payment of debts, fines or marriage cattle—which are recognised as group matters.

In all these concerns people have a claim only upon their lineage kin. But affinal kin can also be useful allies, and what a marriage does is to create an alliance linking two lineages through the woman who is the daughter in one and the wife in the other. Hence it is important for daughters to 'marry well' for more vital reasons than the snobbish ones that were associated with the phrase in Victorian England. Where societies are stratified, snobbish values also play their part; every father who can will ally himself with men of higher status than his own.

When we look back upon the dynastic marriages of earlier centuries in Europe, or the unions by which hereditary aristocracies added land to land and title to title, we readily see that where the links created by marriage are an important element in political structure, the choice of partner cannot be treated as a purely personal matter. It would be going too far

to say that in old-time Africa every marriage was based on
political calculation. Some fathers were not in a position to
indulge ambitions. But the essential point is that in any society
where the most important relationships are based on kinship,
the effects which a marriage will have in the wider field of kin
have to be taken into consideration. It has been said that in
such societies a woman is a 'negotiable good'. This can be con-
ceded if it is recognised that she is so only in relation to the
man who is her guardian in virtue of kinship; she is definitely
not a commodity in common circulation. One might say that
women are pawns in a game of power politics played on a very
small scale; but after all, few fathers are wholly indifferent to
their daughters' interests, and an arranged marriage is not
inevitably a distasteful one.

Contrasts with Western Values

In Europe the theme of the romantic marriage in defiance of
parental wishes is almost as old as the theme of the romantic
love for the unattainable lady. If the first expresses recognition
that the suitable marriage is sometimes irksome, the second
asserts that the ideal union belongs to a different world from
that of every day. It was only in the nineteenth century that
romantic love began to be considered both necessary and un-
assailable as a reason why two persons should marry. This
would hardly have been possible except in conditions of greatly
increased social mobility such as were created by the industrial
revolution. But romantic love became an element in the ideal of
marriage and the family that Christian missionaries taught their
converts. Christian missions have been active in all colonial
territories and most independent ones. Only a minority has
accepted their teaching, but to that minority it has given an
additional argument for that rejection of family controls which
new economic opportunities have made practicable. But the
missionary argument, like most militant arguments, does not
merely advocate its own values as good; it also seeks to dis-
credit those which it opposes, and it does so in this case by
insisting on the hardship which arranged marriages impose on
girls.

78

One cannot leave the matter there without asking whether there were, in fact, no ways in which young people could express their own wishes, and whether parents always disregarded these and inevitably, in pursuing their own interests, injured those of their children. Obviously, the answer must have been different among different peoples. Quite recently cases were reported from the Nyoro, in Uganda, of the suicide of girls who were forced to marry husbands not of their choice. But we read of parents in other parts of Africa giving way to threats of suicide, or of elopements which force the parents' hands; among many peoples courtship precedes marriage and the parents only ratify the young people's choice; it is almost universal for the woman to be required to give her formal consent, for what this is worth, and since it is taken for granted by all girls, except those in the new middle classes, that it is their destiny to be married and that marriage with whatever husband is the prelude to a life of hard work, many of them are content to accept their parents' choice. Hardship is felt where parents oppose a choice that has already been made, or where a girl is obliged to marry a much older man.

But it must be remembered that freedom of choice in marriage and the independence of a young couple are very different things. To have willingly accepted her husband does not by itself exempt a girl from the status of the youngest newcomer in a large composite household of the type that is characteristic of so many pre-industrial societies; the sufferings of the daughter-in-law are a theme of Chinese novel and African proverb alike, and no crusade has been launched to alleviate them.

In contrasting the ideas about marriage that are current in pre-industrial and in industrialised societies, it would be a gross over-simplification to talk as if there were only two opposed conceptions. There are differences in the marriage rules of the pre-industrial societies, and in the industrialised ones competing values are current simultaneously; in countries which nominally adhere to the Christian religion there is a considerable divergence between the rules imposed by the State and those imposed by the Church. In territories which have been subject to colonial rule these conceptions are in competition with traditional values.

But certain broad contrasts can be drawn. In industrialised societies marriage is optional; an unmarried person is not an object of particular remark, nor does he or she suffer any material disadvantage. In subsistence societies marriage is the normal condition for an adult person; in some cases it is post-poned to a fairly late age, particularly by men, but whether to marry at all is not a matter of choice. No man can attain to full adult status without marriage; an independent household can only be maintained by the joint activities of husband and wife. Women in a sense are always minors, since a woman must always be under the guardianship of some man; but women regard marriage and child-bearing as the life for which their whole girlhood has been a preparation. Not all African peoples express their views as forcibly as do the Guisii of Kenya, who say that a woman should not grow grey hairs in her father's home, and believe that disaster befalls a household if a grown daughter dies there. Most of them expect to keep in closer touch with their kinswomen who have married than such statements would imply. But all expect their daughters to marry.

Marriage in Matrilineal Societies

Where descent is matrilineal, the significance of marriage is different. Children belong to their mother's lineage in any case. Men marry not to secure legitimate offspring, but to establish a household; and it is probably significant that in the marriage procedures of matrilineal peoples the payment made plays relatively a much smaller part. Among the Ashanti in Ghana, for example, a suitor is expected to make quite expensive presents to the relatives of his prospective bride and to herself when he is seeking their good-will, but at the sealing of the legal contract all that is paid is the equivalent of the drink which, according to Ashanti custom, should be shared by the parties and the ancestors whenever any agreement is ratified.

Most other matrilineal peoples in Africa include in their marriage ceremonial some specific gift or payment by the husband to his wife's guardian, which is regarded as the essential indication that the marriage has been contracted in due form. The economic value of this payment varies widely among different peoples, and it has been suggested that it is greater where the husband is allowed to take his wife away from her parents' home as soon as they are married; though, as will be seen, payments tend to rise as people enter into the cash economy, so that one cannot be sure what significance to attach to these comparisons. But the part which the payment plays in the creation and maintenance of affinal relationships is far less important than it is where descent is patrilineal.

The ideal for a man, in a matrilineal as in a patrilineal society, is to have an independent household of which he is the head. The arrangement which is most common in the matrilineal societies, however, is for the wife to stay with her own people during at least the first years of married life. Among the Ashanti the husband also lives with his maternal kin, and the food which his wife cooks for him in her home is sent for him to eat in his. But in the so-called 'matrilineal' belt which stretches across the Congo through Northern Rhodesia and Nyasaland to Tanganyika, a young husband lives with his wife at her mother's village until her male guardian agrees to let him take her away. It appears that among the Bemba a man expects to live among his wife's people until he himself has married daughters, and only then moves away, taking his daughters and their husbands with him to found a village of which he will be the head. But in Nyasaland it is regarded as correct to let the husband take his wife away from the control of her kinsmen after her first child is born. By this time he is supposed to have been able to demonstrate whether his character is such that his wife can safely be entrusted to his sole care. But if her kinsmen are not satisfied of this, and refuse their consent, the husband does not necessarily stay meekly where he is. He is much more likely to leave his wife, and this, indeed, may be what she and her relatives intend.

It has generally been observed that divorce is frequent in matrilineal societies. Nevertheless, the ideal of marriage as a continuing relationship exists, and matrilineal peoples do lay upon kinsmen the duty of intervention in matrimonial disputes.

In their case it is not having received cattle that lays this obligation upon them, but having been expressly nominated as 'marriage sureties'. Each party has two sureties, usually a brother and a kinsman of the parental generation; sometimes the senior man of a lineage is the senior surety for the marriages of all its members. If either spouse has a complaint, it must be taken to the marriage surety of the other, and the agreement of all four sureties is necessary for the dissolution of a marriage.

Where children belong to the line of their mother, the desire of the lineage for progeny is expressed in the feeling, not that it is a woman's duty to bear children, but that it is her right; this notion is not absent among patrilineal peoples, but it might perhaps be described as dominant in matrilineal societies. 'Fertility', one writer has put it, 'is a precious but time-limited gift which must be used or it will be wasted'.[1] A woman is expected to be faithful to a husband who lives with her, but the idea that she should remain barren because he is absent is considered absurd. This attitude is significant in those societies where the men are accustomed to be away from home for long periods working for wages. It leads, in some circumstances, to the condonation of adultery among patrilineal peoples; in matrilineal ones in the same circumstances it simply leads to divorce and re-marriage.

Marriage in Changing Africa

The entry of Africa into the world society, and the introduction to it of foreign codes of ethics and of law, have inevitably influenced these close-knit systems which depend for their essential character on permanent contact between people in small local groupings. African kinship and family systems have been affected, not only by the creation of new economic opportunities which reduce the mutual interdependence of members of kin groups, and by the fact that people often have to travel long distances to take advantage of these opportunities, but by the introduction of new laws which are held by their makers to embody high moral standards, by the direct teaching of

1. E. Colson, *Marriage and the Family among the Plateau Tonga*, 1958, p. 154

Christian missions, and also by the example of a new type of household organisation which is not only held up as a model but has been associated with the dominant group in a new social and political order.

The nature of the changes that take place depends on the way in which the general environment of the people concerned is changing; if they stay in their own homes and take to commercial production, the most significant changes will not be the same as those that occur when the younger men are away working for wages for a large part of their time, while those who stay at home are still occupied only in providing their own subsistence; and they will be different again among populations which have migrated to urban areas or even overseas.

An example was quoted from Ghana of the extended family household working as an economic unit. For a picture of a society that was once equally firmly based on patrilineal kinship, but has been largely transformed in the course of the last sixty years, we may look to the Ngoni of Northern Rhodesia as they have been described by Barnes.[1] The Ngoni might be considered a special case, since in addition to the forces which colonial rule have everywhere brought into play, a factor in their development has been that they live among matrilineal populations who were once their subjects. Nevertheless, they illustrate most of the changes in kinship and family structure that have taken place in colonial populations which have come to depend on a cash income derived from wage labour.

For much of the nineteenth century the Ngoni were the dominant tribe in a considerable part of what is now north-eastern Rhodesia and Nyasaland. They had built up their state in the course of a northward journey from their original home in Zululand which took some seventy years. In every country that they passed through they raided cattle and took captives. The captives were attached to the following of leading warriors and thus incorporated into the Ngoni organisation, those who entered it earlier coming to have higher rank.

The Ngoni who settled in the present Fort Jameson area lived in very large villages, subdivided into homesteads where

1. *Marriage in a Changing Society*, Rhodes–Livingstone Paper 20, 1951

two or three close patrilineal kin dwelt together much as has been described in the case of the Tallensi. Each village had at some time been placed under the control of a lieutenant of the Paramount Chief, who had appointed his kinsmen or dependants (the descendants of his captives) to exercise authority over sections of it. All these offices were hereditary in the male line, and no one could repudiate his allegiance to the political superior of his own division, or take up residence in any other than that to which he belonged by birth. Thus an important effect of the marriage rules, which were those that have been described as characteristic of a patrilineal system with cattle payment, was to fix the local as well as the kinship unit to which every male child would belong throughout his life. As Barnes puts it, 'The function of marriage was, in this context, to locate children in the system unambiguously and unequivocally.'

The peoples from whom the most recent captives had been taken were the Cewa, who, like most of the indigenous peoples of this area, were matrilineal and so recognised different marriage rules. While they were under the direct control of the Ngoni they appear to have been made to follow Ngoni marriage laws.

When the Ngoni were defeated by the British in 1898, their villages were burned and many of their cattle looted. They scattered into the bush, only close kinsmen remaining together. Later they began to join into larger villages, but the long-established hereditary structure of the old days had been destroyed, and it probably could not have been re-created even if the Paramount Chief and his lieutenant had wished to attempt this. But since they were no longer able to make war on their neighbours, the *raison d'être* of their former close organisation was gone.

The most recently incorporated Cewa sections now separated themselves from the Ngoni and returned to the neighbouring tribes to which they belonged. But later, as land was alienated for European farms, Cewa began to come back and establish their own villages among the Ngoni. Headmen appointed by the government were given authority over these villages, and since every headman sought to have men in his village, anyone could live where he pleased. Thus patrilineal descent ceased to be the principle by which residence and political allegiance were decided. And at the same time it had become impossible for any Ngoni to offer marriage cattle.

All these are special features, the result of the historical accidents that the migrations of the Ngoni led them into the homes of matrilineal peoples and that their conquerors deprived them of their cattle. They also had the experience that they share with the great majority of the population of Africa, of being induced or required to seek employment far from their homes—in their case in Southern Rhodesia or on building the railway line.

Here, as nearly everywhere that anthropologists have worked, the older generation lament that marriage is not what it used to be, that wives are unfaithful and that divorce is frequent. Since anthropologists began collecting records of marriages and divorces and correlating them with the age of the people concerned, they have become chary of taking these statements at their face value. It is pretty clear that the fidelity of wives in the old days was not as ideal as all that. But it is clear too that the long absences of the husbands who go away to earn wages create a situation that did not exist in the days of the subsistence economy.

The remarkable feature in the development of marriage law among the Ngoni, however, is that it is no longer based on the idea that what matters is to determine the kinship status of children. What is considered important now is to determine the marital status of women, and this for reasons which were not of great significance in the old days. A payment in cash, which is called not by the old Ngoni name for the cattle payment, but by a word taken from the matrilineal Cewa, gives a man the right to damages if his wife commits adultery. It is also the evidence of marriage required by the Native Authorities who, as servants of the government, issue marriage certificates when these are asked for; and the main significance of a marriage certificate is to establish a claim to the accommodation, free transport, etc, which some employers allow to the wives of their employees.

In the eyes of the contemporary Ngoni, however, there is no

one act which marks the distinction between a legal marriage and mere cohabitation. People who cannot afford it are considered to be excused from making payments, and it is a matter for the general judgment of their neighbours whether a couple are to be regarded as married or as 'just friends'. There is a borderline category described by a term which Barnes translates as 'poorly fixed marriages'. These are unions which are not expected to last in view of the character of the parties, but which are nevertheless awarded the title of marriage. If such a union does last, it may come to be regarded as a proper marriage; if it breaks up, this may be taken as proof that it was never really a marriage. The practical question here is whether the woman's parents recognise the man's marital rights over their daughter, and this will depend on whether he behaves to them as a son-in-law should, and particularly whether he has formally approached them at the outset.

According to Ngoni traditions divorce was very rare in the old days, and this was one of their grounds for considering themselves superior to their matrilineal neighbours. There is therefore no record of any formal obligation on kinsmen to mediate in matrimonial quarrels and use their influence to keep the marriage in being. But the principal reason why divorce is sought today is not dissension within the household but the long absence of the husband, and for this no traditional peacemaking methods provide a remedy. This is the social side of the dilemma of the peoples in 'labour-reservoir' areas; the maintenance which wives today expect includes goods that their husbands can only provide by earning money, but they also expect their husbands to give them children and not let their precious fertility be wasted. As it has been put in a neighbouring tribe, 'A woman marries a man and not a blanket.' Moreover, though some husbands regularly send presents and money home, others do not; they find that it costs more than they expected to live in town, or they lose money gambling, or they form a relationship with a woman there and spend their earnings on her. Thus, both wives and their relatives often have every inducement to terminate a marriage if a new prospective husband appears.

However, this is no longer regarded as merely a matter to be settled between the kinsmen of the parties. Two organisations of wider scale now claim a voice—the State and the Church. Christian missions have laid the main emphasis of their teaching on the type of family life which their converts should lead, and in particular on the sanctity and finality of the marriage vow. Some of them will allow the divorce of a deserted wife, others will not countenance the re-marriage of a woman unless the death of her husband can be proved.

The State in this context is represented by the Native Authorities—hereditary chiefs with their councillors, who are given responsibility by the Protectorate Government for the maintenance of law and order and the judging of cases concerning matters covered by native custom. In these courts divorce can be effected by the agreement of the couple and the kin responsible for them, but dispute may arise over the return of the legalisation payment, if this has been made. Only the native court can award damages for adultery. Hence a large number of cases are brought before the courts. The ideal upheld by the courts is the same as that of the missions, namely, that marriages should be kept in being; and although they recognise more reasons for holding this to be impossible than the missions do, they nevertheless throw their weight against divorce.

In a case quoted by Barnes a woman was refused divorce although she claimed that her husband beat her and that she had to go to hospital. One of the councillors said that it was not the work of the court to force men and women to divorce one another but to instruct them how to live together in peace! This is the kind of case in which an administrative officer reviewing the court records might take the line that the woman had been hardly done by; anyhow Ngoni councillors believe that they have to grant divorces only because the government requires it.

A very interesting feature of the contemporary situation is that those men who do still make a payment that is regarded as the equivalent of the cattle payment are more likely to make it at the time when they are divorced than at any other. Thus the Ngoni illustrate as few other people do the distinction between rights over a wife and rights over her children. Both are combined in most marriages, but the difference in emphasis in the two types of right is the essential element in the different attitudes towards marriage in societies which are and are not based on patriliny. As a result of historical accident the Ngoni now recognise two separate payments as creating these separate rights. Nowadays it is only when a man loses his wife that he is afraid of losing his claims over her children; that is that they will choose not to live in his village when they grow up. Even the making of the payment only imposes upon them a moral obligation which no authority can enforce.

Although some of the most interesting features of this situation are peculiar to the Ngoni, it does illustrate a process which can be seen to be generally at work, since the essential reason for most of the new developments is that African peoples have been incorporated into a wider society in which other relationships take the place of those created by kinship. A man can live where he likes because he does not depend primarily upon his kinsmen for his economic prospects or for securing his legal rights; he gets the first from wage labour, growing cash crops, trading or some small-scale craft such as carpentry or repairing bicycles, and the second from a wide-scale legal system that does not allow resort to force.

Such a complete destruction of traditional organisation as Barnes has described is not common in rural Africa; it has not happened among peoples who were not subdued by force, or even among some, such as the Tallensi, who were. But the closest ties of kinship are everywhere being loosened, and everywhere this can be traced to the new opportunities of earning money. The quarrels among the Tallensi over the disposal of resources which in theory are held in common have been mentioned. When resources consist in livestock, they cannot be concealed, but when they consist in money it is easy to hide them. Moreover, the possession of money makes people independent; young men can now make their own marriage payments, and it was for this above all that they used to depend upon their elders. Tallensi say that nowadays, if a father tries to assert his authority over a disrespectful son, the son will simply go off to work for wages. Elsewhere this is an escape from arduous kinds of work, such as the herding which falls to the lot of a Fulani youth.

The substitution of cash for ceremonial payments such as that made at marriage has introduced a new mercenary element into the relationships where gifts are called for. Fathers are just as anxious to keep money that they should distribute among their kinsmen as are sons to keep money that they should hand over to their fathers. Moreover, even if a cash payment is distributed in the same way that the cattle payment was, it does not have the same effect as a reminder of obligations, for cash is spent and forgotten. Arguments as to what payments are returnable, and whether some particular amount of money represented the marriage payment proper or one of the incidental gifts, are common.

While it is true that in some African societies there were significant differences of wealth even in the subsistence economy, and that wealthy men, who were also aristocrats, were often expected to give more cattle when their sons married, the inequalities were not so wide. Now there is more freedom for fathers to seek suitors who will bring a large sum, while the less self-seeking motives for controlling their daughters' marriages have lost weight with the decline in importance of the wider kin group. The amount of the payment expected is everywhere increasing, despite many efforts that have been made to limit it by law.

Legal Marriage as a Status Symbol

Some twenty years ago it was found that among the Ganda, as among the Ngoni, many couples omitted to go through the recognised formalities of marriage. One reason here was the high cash payment which had come to be expected. Another was the fact that the native courts, which here are more strongly under mission influence than in any other part of Africa, do not recognise any other marriage than one made in church, and so will not deal with demands for the return of the payment. But there is also at work the factor which has been noted as significant among the Ngoni, the dispersal of kin groups. The cause of this is quite different in Buganda. It is that land has been allocated in freehold tenure and people live where they choose to buy or rent land; if they rent it as tenants, they may move often from one place to another. To disregard the formalities of marriage is not to repudiate the rules; it is seen rather as the postponement of an action which circumstances make difficult.

But alongside the traditional marriage procedure there exists now everywhere the one that has been introduced by the missions. This is held, as it is in the countries from which the missionaries come, to include, in addition to the religious blessing of the union, conspicuous consumption on a considerable scale—special garments for bride, bridegroom and bridesmaids, a wedding photograph, a car to transport the bridal party, perhaps printed invitation cards, and a feast afterwards. The cost of such a wedding may be more than the marriage payment itself, and it is often asserted that as a result of it many young couples start their married life in debt. Yet the outlay is considered necessary because it is an assertion of the attainment of a new social status, that of the educated minority who aspire to the Western way of life as it has been shown them by their teachers. Marriage in European style is the distinguishing mark of members of this class.

Here we have a situation parallel with what has been observed in the field of social change in the Caribbean. There is one very obvious difference between this area and all the others that are considered in this book; that instead of organised societies living in their own territory, we are concerned with populations of mixed origin whose ancestors a few generations back were taken by force from their homes and dispersed in a manner far more drastic than anything experienced in Africa itself.

Some writers have seen in the state of slavery itself, and in the fact that slaves were not allowed to marry, factors predisposing to the present state of affairs, in which a large number of unions have no legal sanction and a high percentage of births are illegitimate. I would suggest as an alternative explanation that, just as among the Fort Jameson Ngoni, there are now no corporate kin groups interested in the control of marriage, and that the only marriage procedure recognised is that which is also taken to be the hall-mark of middle class status. A legal marriage implies more than its legal consequences; it implies in particular that the woman will not be expected to contribute anything towards the expenses of the household. Hence, only men with a secure income can embark upon it.

But the explanation has been developed yet further by R. T. Smith in a study of the rural family in British Guiana.[1] He shows, in effect, that in the modern Caribbean family the position of the father is marginal, as it is in the matrilineal family of Central Africa—but *not* because the Negroes of the Caribbean have a tradition of matrilineal descent. The reason lies in the structure of modern Caribbean society, in which, as in Central Africa, though for very different reasons, the status of the family is not tied to that of the father. In Central Africa it is membership of a matrilineal descent group that fixes an individual's place in his society. In the Caribbean this is fixed by the total structure of an ethnically stratified society which assigns the Negroes to the lowest level. Within this system there is room for a certain amount of mobility. A minority of the Negro population enter government service and the professions, and so move from the lower to the middle class; they carry their families with them, and such families are based on legal marriage, with the permanency and the assumption of the father's status by the children that this implies.

In the majority of rural families—for even in the villages there are one or two persons of higher status—the father's position confers no particular advantage upon his children, nor are they dependent on him any more than upon their mother, since the meagre opportunities of earning which exist are open to women as much as to men.

Marriage in Singapore
For Chinese who have emigrated to Singapore, the changes in the structure of the family and kin group have been of a

1. *The Negro Family in British Guiana*, 1956

different nature.[1] In contrast to the Negro populations of the Caribbean, the Chinese of Singapore are relatively recent arrivals. An emigrant may keep up relations with his kin in China by sending money home or occasionally by visits, but when he is dead his children will not remember them, and cousins in Singapore may be unknown to one another. People remember their village of origin, but in Singapore there is no place that belongs to the village, nor any corporate activities in which its members unite, and there is no founding of lineages by the emigrants. Circumstances do not allow large bodies of kin to live in one locality—people find housing where they can—and it seems that for a body of kin to become a cohesive group they must have some home ground as a basis. For the help in crises which the lineage gave in so many rural societies, Singapore Chinese—in this like so many immigrants to towns in Africa—look to associations of persons of common geographical origin but not recognising traceable kinship.

The Singapore Chinese family differs from the Caribbean family in that it is expected to be constituted by a legal marriage and is indisputably under the authority of the father, though the efforts of colonial law to incorporate Chinese traditional custom have resulted in considerable confusion as to how a legal marriage is created. One can see here the significance of the contrast between Singapore, with its range of economic opportunities for Chinese and consequent extreme social mobility, and British Guiana with its stratification by colour and limited opportunities for Negroes.

Although, as has been shown, membership of a wider kin group has lost its significance in Singapore as it has in most great cities, the other function of legally recognised paternity mentioned by Smith is of extreme importance here. Singapore society is emphatically of the type in which the status of the family, and with it the chance of attaining yet higher status in the next generation, is determined primarily by the occupation of the father. The tradition of the father's dominance over wife and even adult children has been weakened but by no means destroyed. The most powerful influence against it is, of course,

1. *See* M. Freedman, *Chinese Family and Marriage in Singapore*, 1957

the transition from an economy where a high proportion of the household requirements are produced by the family in co-operation and its scanty income comes from the sale of produce, arranged by the head, to one in which each member independently sells his labour and receives a cash income from a different source. Whereas among the Tallensi, at the time when Fortes described them, the wages earned by the younger men were supplementary to the products of family labour, in Singapore the dependence on cash is complete, and the necessity for co-operation between the members, and so for the recognition of the senior man's authority, is absent. Further, the educated Chinese are very consciously aware that 'modern' ideas oppose the old-fashioned ideal of the family and favour the independence of both wives and children. These modern ideas, although they are Western in origin, have been seen by the overseas Chinese not as those of alien imperialists, but as those of reforming political movements in the Chinese homeland.

As Freedman has neatly put it in his description of modern-style marriage ceremonies, it is not the long-established Chinese population, but the most recent immigrants, who 'brought orange-blossom with their Mandarin and bouquets with their nationalism'. Changes in the traditional marriage laws of China were imposed by Chinese governments in 1931 and have doubtless been carried further by the Communist régime. But it is notoriously hard to influence family relationships by legislation, and if one is following out the process by which they change, one is more likely to find explanations in changes in the circumstances which make family unity necessary.

Change in Matrilineal Societies

Most of the illustrations which have been given so far have been taken from patrilineal societies. But matrilineal societies have problems of their own in the changing situation.

In these societies a woman bears children for her own lineage and not for her husband's, and since heritable property is passed down the line of kin, it cannot go from father to son.

93

But such property is still held by men; the difference is that a man's heir is the son of his sister. Yet the family of father, mother and children form an economic unit, working their fields and consuming the produce together, and the father is expected to see that the wife and children are provided with such goods as are made by men. He builds their house, and in the old days he made their clothes of beaten bark or raffia mats; today he is expected to earn money to clothe them, and also to pay for the children's schooling if they go to school. He could be divorced for failing to meet the first obligation, but not for neglecting the second, since schooling is still a luxury in most African villages. Thus it is erroneous to suppose, as is sometimes done in missionary circles, that in a matrilineal system a father takes no responsibility for his children. He does not, however, have the final authority over them; the mother's brother has a claim on their services, which he may exercise in such a way as to keep them from school. It has also been said of some of the peoples of Nyasaland that a man has no right to chastise his own child but must appeal to his wife's brother; and certainly men are sometimes treated in a very off-hand way by their wives' brothers. But most men who, as husbands and fathers, suffer these indignities, are in a position to inflict them in turn on the husbands of their sisters; and as time goes on, of their daughters. In most matrilineal societies a man eventually becomes able to establish a household in which he is master.

Although some old-fashioned theorists assumed that patriliny was everywhere established by a revolt of males against the indignities of matriliny, such matrilineal systems as exist in Africa today do not seem to have been found intolerable until European penetration brought with it new ways of accumulating wealth. For the Akan peoples of Ghana and the Ivory Coast, the new source of income was cocoa farming; in this a man often worked with his sons, and the sons, very naturally, were not willing on his death to hand over the farm to their cousins.

For the matrilineal peoples of Central Africa there is not often much money to be made in farming; there the way to

94

make an income above the average is as a clerk, teacher, or medical dresser, or an artisan. Such activities almost inevitably take men away from their home village and from contact with their wider circle of kin. They may build themselves brick houses; an artisan will have his tools, a trader his stock. Thir children will grow up at the standard of living, at least a little higher than that of the village, which their father's activities have made possible. If their father has a trade, he may teach it to them. Yet, if the traditional rules are followed, when he dies they must hand over house, tools and stock to someone they have never seen. In the popular stereotyped picture of such a situation, the sons would have used their father's tools whereas the nephew 'just sells them'. I have heard this said even of a bicycle, though there can be few Africans who would not use a bicycle. It has been remarked that such a system of inheritance leads to no trouble in a homogeneous society producing its own subsistence, since no man leaves conspicuously more property than anyone else. But when there are marked differences in wealth it begins to break down. This may be one reason why cattle people are nearly always patrilineal.

But we do not, of course, find that people turn over from the large matrilineal kin group to the large patrilineal kin group. What we find in the rural areas is that systems based on descent in either line are giving way to looser arrangements in which, though people still like to live near others who are in some way related to them, there is no pressure to choose one particular category of kin. This is clearly related to the fact that people no longer depend upon their kin for their most important economic resources, for defence against attack, or for securing their rights. The labour market now supplies the first function of the kin group, and a political system which commands a monopoly of force the others.

CHAPTER 4

NEW STATES

*African political systems—Colonial rule—Changes in the
balance of power—The 'good chief' in African and European
eyes—The new élites—Chiefs in the new states—Micro-
nationalism—The 'erosion of democracy'.*

THE WORLD OF MODERN TECHNOLOGY is one of large political
units. As new states come into being with the withdrawal of
colonial rule the question sometimes arises whether they are big
enough to stand on their own feet. Such is the pressure of
nationalism that demands for autonomy from very small populations have proved irresistible more often than not; in so far
as such populations are dependent on foreign subsidies they
are not really standing on their own feet, but although they
sometimes talk of entering into unions with their neighbours
there has been very little action in this direction.

Yet of the new African states only the two smallest, Rwanda
and Burundi, were political units in the period before colonial
rule; the only other examples, as it happens, are territories
which at the time of writing are not yet independent—Swazi-
land and Basutoland, each of which recognises a single paramount chief. In all the others there are numbers of peoples
speaking different languages, and very commonly those who do
have a common language are divided into groups which a
century ago were politically autonomous.

It has also happened that frontiers drawn at a time when
nothing was known about the ethnic affiliations of the populations they divided have cut in two a language unit, or even the
area ruled by a single chief. The new states are seeking to

rectify such errors—particularly those which could extend their boundaries by doing so—and their governments usually accompany their claims with denunciations of the 'artificial' frontiers of the colonial era. But all the new states are artificial constructions in exactly this sense; and if their populations had not been artificially—that is by forces acting on them from outside—brought within administrative frameworks wider than any that they had themselves evolved, they could not conceivably have taken the place in the family of nations that they have today.

This process has naturally not left the individual units as they were. The systems of political authority that the colonial powers found in Africa were modified deliberately by the new rulers, and even more profoundly shaken by the indirect consequences of their rule. The assertion or reassertion of independence has not implied the restoration of the earlier systems, but the supersession of a foreign bureaucracy by one manned by Africans, and the introduction of constitutions based on Western models of various kinds, but operated by Africans with their own conception of the way the roles should be played.

This book is concerned not with the conspicuous events that form the chronicle of political history, but rather with the extension of the range of the ordinary person's social relations that modern technology has brought about. In the field of politics this means what government offers him and demands of him, how the offers are implemented and the demands enforced, and what values are invoked to justify the exercise of authority by particular individuals.

African Political Systems

Africa south of the Sahara provides the greatest possible variety of ways in which the first function of government—the maintenance of social order—might be fulfilled. At the time of its partition between colonial powers, there were a few large kingdoms, such as the Emirate of Kano with its population of five million or so, or Buganda with about one million, in addition to a vast number of rulers whose subjects might number anything between half a million and a few thousand. These kingdoms presented to the new rulers something that they could recognise from their knowledge of their own past history—hereditary monarchs making effective through territorial subordinates (yes, even in populations of only four thousand) their authority in dispensing justice, collecting revenue and organising defensive and offensive warfare. Public opinion in Europe, imbued with the Whig tradition or that of 1789, as the case might be, was predisposed to see these monarchs as tyrants concerned only with self-interest, and indeed one of the elements of the 'civilising mission' was conceived as the introduction of a juster and less oppressive rule. British colonial government sought to do this by guiding the rulers in the paths of enlightenment; French ones, more often, by depriving them of political authority.

A different problem was posed by the considerable number of peoples who had no chiefs at all, but were organised in a manner entirely alien to Western notions. These are the societies which have been described as *acephalous*—to indicate the absence of any individual who is recognised as a supreme authority—or *segmentary*—to indicate that they are divided into lineages of equal status, no one of which recognises any authority beyond that of its own senior member. A group of lineages recognises 'the rule of law' in the sense of recognising that between their members rights should be respected and wrongs alone compensated; such a group could be called a political unit. Most such acephalous political units are subdivisions of larger aggregates having a common name, language and customs.[1] Some anthropologists, notably Evans-Pritchard, have used the word *people* for the larger aggregate and *tribe* for the politically autonomous subdivision, and this is one of the few contexts in which the word 'tribe' is used with any precision.

In such societies the rights which are recognised include that of self-help in obtaining redress for injuries. Homicide is avenged, compensation is sought for other offences, and

1. *See* E. E. Evans-Pritchard, *The Nuer*, 1940, and L. P. Mair, *Primitive Government*, 1961

property is seized from a debtor, by the injured party and his friends or kinsmen.

The place of police and courts of justice in securing respect for obligations is taken here by the knowledge that the injured can be expected to fight for their rights. This is an ultimate sanction, just as recourse to police and courts is in the Western world; people respect one another's rights a good deal of the time.

The most turbulent of the acephalous peoples are the foot-loose cattle-owners whose young men spend their time ranging the pastures with their herds and who may, like the Nilotes of the southern Sudan, have to move as a body to the rare water-holes in the dry season and back again to the limited areas that are above flood water in the rains. Those who can live per-manently in one place, grazing their herds near by, such as the peoples of northern Ghana or some of the Kenya Bantu, seem to be readier to settle their differences without a fight—though even with them the settlement is of a diplomatic rather than a judicial nature, agreed between the heads of lineages, not im-posed by any impartial outsider, and sometimes rejected by one of the disputing parties.

To anthropologists there is a rule of law wherever common obligations are recognised and an injury can in principle be made good by the payment of compensation. But administrators with a civilising mission—and I do not use these words with a sneer—have meant by it the obligation to submit disputes to peaceful settlement, and they have not been willing to tolerate breaches of the peace that it is one of their duties to maintain. This is the first point at which colonial rule has modified the political organisation of the acephalous peoples. If, in this context, I refer to civilising missions without a sneer, it is because those African peoples who have chiefs regard the administration of justice as the most valuable activity of a chief, and because there are instances on record of acephalous peoples asking the chief who ruled over their neighbours to give them one of his sons to settle their disputes.

Another type of acephalous organisation is that based on age; this was traditionally characteristic of many of the peoples of Kenya. In such a system the whole male population share in political functions—as fighters when they are young, as judges, councillors and priests when they are old. Individuals of commanding personality have influence in proportion, as such people do in any society, but there is no office carrying superior authority with it. Where the *raison d'être* of age organisation is preparation for war, it has naturally been frowned upon by the overlords whose function it was to maintain internal peace within the area which they have constituted as a single political unit, and for political purposes it ceased to exist as soon as foreign administration was made effective.

Colonial Rule

The essence of the new situation that was created by colonial rule was the need of the new overlords for intermediaries between themselves and the mass of the population. Where travelling is slow and difficult and the majority of the population is illiterate, the execution of government policies must depend upon direct contact to a degree that is hard for Westerners to picture. Governments need an administrative staff distributed throughout their territory, who will both make known and enforce the new laws and obligations which they find it necessary to impose. The lowest ranks of this organisation must of necessity belong to the indigenous population.

A great deal of nonsense is currently talked about a supposed system, or philosophy, called 'Indirect Rule', which is rarely defined or even described by the people who do the talking, but which actually means giving administrative responsibility to traditional rulers. In the period between the two world wars it was widely supposed that Britain had invented 'Indirect Rule', and in so doing had found the key to the administration of 'backward peoples' and their introduction to Western values without undue disturbance of their own. In this sense it could have been called a philosophy, and it was much more than a system. Since the end of the second world war it has been equally widely supposed that Britain invented 'Indirect Rule', but now the received idea is that this disastrous device is responsible for most of the problems that the new African states have to contend with. Books on Africa are apt to contain in an early chapter the statement that Britain, by adopting the policy of 'Indirect Rule', and so recognising the distinctness of different African peoples, failed to create a sense of nationhood in whatever territory is under discussion.[1] The problem of the 'sense of nationhood' certainly calls for discussion. It is because there is no such sense in Kenya that a constitution has had to be devised for that country giving a large measure of autonomy to each of six different regions. But whatever may be the reason for this, it cannot have been the recognition of traditional rulers, for in Kenya there were no traditional rulers, and local administration was carried on by British officials with the advice of councils partly elected and partly nominated.

The crucial fact is that in a centralised political system the superior authorities must have some identifiable individuals at every level of the administrative hierarchy who can receive instructions and be held responsible for their execution. These have been chosen in different ways, depending in part on who was available and in part on the views of the colonial authorities as to the right kind of person to choose. Whatever their theoretical preconceptions, the rulers have always had to consider both the need for at least a minimum of bureaucratic efficiency and the need for choosing as their intermediaries persons who commanded obedience for some other reason than the backing of the foreign power. Some sort of compromise has had to be sought, or choice made, between aims which have at times proved incompatible.

Where no single individual commands obedience, the agent of the colonial power must be arbitrarily chosen: someone who, as a police or army sergeant, has held some responsibility, has perhaps learned to read and write, and has got some idea of the kind of actions that the colonial authority is interested in encouraging and repressing.

Where local tradition does accord authority to an individual, the question is whether the new responsibilities shall be entrusted to him or to someone else. At this point it is necessary

1. *See* e.g., H. and M. Smythe, *The New Nigerian Elite*, 1960

to reflect that conquerors throughout the ages have established their position by reducing conquered rulers to the status of tributaries. Indeed, where the main aim of conquest is tribute this is the obvious thing to do; rulers who already have their own organisation for the collection of revenues are simply required to hand over part of what they collect to the conqueror. The problem is more complicated if the conquerors make it their business to introduce new laws and a new system of values. Nevertheless, the idea of employing recognised rulers as agents of a new authority is one of the least original in history.

In Africa the difference between the major colonial powers in this respect has been one of degree. All have imposed new responsibilities on traditional authorities, and have grouped together units which have been independent at the time when they came under European rule. Some have been readier than others to substitute for traditional rulers men of the type whom they had to employ where there was no ruler; in West Africa the French employed many men who had learnt French at school and acted as interpreters. The French not only amalgamated small autonomous units under a single chief (either the chief of one part of the new chiefdom or an ex-interpreter) but created *cantons*, as they were called, with boundaries that had no relation to existing ethnic divisions. For some reason, to have created 'artificial frontiers' within a territory is not included by the critics of colonialism in the list of its offences; some critics would, it seems, count it an offence to have avoided doing so.

The distinctive features of British policy were, in fact (1) that they maintained the unity of existing ethnic groups, though sometimes combining these in units of quasi-federal type; (2) that where a hereditary office of chief was recognised they appointed as Native Authorities persons with a traditional claim to this office; (3) that they assigned revenues to each Native Authority for expenditure within its area; (4) that, in the last period of their rule, they sought to democratise the Native Authorities by attaching representative councils to them. Only in a few cases, where traditional rulers had their own subordinate hierarchy and through it controlled populations of considerable size, did these rulers in fact continue to exercise any significant degree of authority independent of external control.

But the internal changes which colonial rule brought to African societies were necessarily different according as it implied the creation of new offices or the modification of existing ones. In the acephalous societies individuals were endowed with authority of a kind that these societies had not known before, deriving its support not from local values but from their relationship with the new rulers. Even within these societies the effect of creating 'chiefs' or 'headmen' was different in different circumstances, one of these being how much administering the superior power actually sought to do.

An example of a nearly unadministrable people are the Turkana of north-western Kenya, nomad herdsmen who move in small bands in search of such water and grazing as the capricious rainfall of their country provides.[1] The disastrous droughts of 1960 and 1961 made of a terrain that is near desert at the best of times a literal desert, and depleted their stock to a point where they found themselves driven to recoup by raiding their neighbours.

In the era of optimism and ten-year plans that followed the end of the second world war there was talk of controlling grazing areas in some attempt to conserve, and perhaps improve, the limited pastoral resources of Turkanaland, but it was always clear that the country would not lend itself to any extensive development schemes. Hence administration has meant the bare minimum of preventing people, as far as possible, from raiding other people's cattle, and collecting the tax which the Turkana were able to raise by selling some of their livestock.

Neither of these functions was delegated to any Turkana. Cases were heard at the District Commissioner's office, and he travelled through the country at the appropriate season to receive tax payments. But there had to be somebody who, in his absence, could exhort people to adopt the new method of settling their quarrels, warn them when the time for paying tax was coming, and report to the District Commissioner breaches

1. See P. H. Gulliver, *A Preliminary Survey of the Turkana*, 1951

of the peace and crises such as epidemics which called for action by the authorities. 'Headmen' were nominated by the administration to perform these duties; they were chosen for two qualities which were not necessarily always combined in one person—local prestige and some comprehension of the aims of Government; men who had served in the police, or as interpreters, were credited with the latter quality. Perhaps fifty headmen were appointed.

These headmen saw the District Commissioner only when he travelled through the country, as he did annually for the tax collection and at other times as occasion called for or permitted. It rested with them to be zealous or otherwise in his absence, and most of them were not very zealous. Moreover, they were required to stay in the same place, and that a place where a messenger from the District Commissioner could easily reach them; so that they were not in close touch with the nomadic Turkana.

Changes in the Balance of Power

Nevertheless the appointment of these headmen introduced a new factor into the social relations of the Turkana. This was not because of their political relationship with the Kenya authorities, but because they were the first Turkana to have a regular cash income. Small as this was[1] it gave these few men economic resources which their fellows did not have, and enabled them to buy those imported goods—pots and pans, matches, cotton garments—the possession of which is a source of prestige as well as of practical convenience. Some of them have been able to build up herds by buying animals outside Turkanaland, and some have been clever enough to buy up their neighbours' cattle cheap when cash was needed for tax payment.

Turkanaland is not the only place where the establishment of a centralised government with Western ideas of administration has created a new social class with a standard of living above the average. But it can be regarded as a limiting case because elsewhere the chiefs appointed by colonial governments

1. 50s a month in 1950

have in fact carried out administrative duties, and because elsewhere the generality of the population have also been able to earn money incomes.

In choosing local agents of their administration colonial governments have sometimes had, as among the Turkana, to create authority out of nothing, but often they have found in existence chiefs with a claim to command obedience. Some colonial rulers, notably the French, have disregarded these as far as possible, though even they have found that there were some rulers whom they could not bypass and were not prepared to destroy by force. But it is the line of least resistance to operate through existing authorities where they can be found, and they can be found in the great majority of the small-scale societies, even though their range is sometimes very narrow.

When someone who has been exercising paramount authority is reduced to the status of agent of an external power, the balance of his relationship with his own subjects is altered— how much, depends upon how extensive was his independent rule. Under colonial rule all African chiefs lost both the right and the power to make war, and their right to use coercive force against their own subjects was very much curtailed. For some this meant that the support of the new rulers was now the main source of their power. But a few were at the head of states so organised that they did not lose the original sources of their power, and in relationships with them the new rulers had to walk warily, and seek a co-operation that they were not in a position to demand.

The most conspicuous examples of this latter type are the Emirates of Northern Nigeria in the west, and the kingdom of Buganda in the east, of Africa. All these were initially brought under British rule by conquest, and all, as it happens, by the same man, Frederick Lugard. The Emirs were required to give up raiding their neighbours' territory for slaves or allowing their subjects to do so. Those who refused were deposed, and those who agreed did not conspicuously break their word; they understood that this was something the new rulers were prepared to suppress by force of arms. But in other respects they were far too firmly established, with their own hierarchy of

loyal subordinates controlling populations running into millions
and the whole system sanctioned by the principles of Islam, to
be coerced by mere disapproval in directions in which they
did not want to move. Criticism of the failure of British
adminstrations to modernise the Emirates does not allow
sufficiently for this balance of power.

In the kingdom of Buganda a progressive governor sought to
hasten the process of modernisation by the exercise of his
prerogatives. From 1950 onwards it was British policy in
Africa to create representative legislatures in preparation for
the grant of independence. The Kabaka of Buganda refused
to let his country participate in such a legislature representing
the whole of Buganda; the Ganda would be a minority in the
total number, and he was not willing to accept this status for
his country. After a period of difficult negotiations the governor
decided that there was nothing for it but to withdraw recognition from the Kabaka and depose him from his throne. Now
the Ganda were not unanimous in their attitude towards
representation in the legislature, nor in their feelings towards
the Kabaka; but they did feel such indignation at the treatment
of the ruler who was the symbol of their nation that he had to
be restored before discussions of political advance could go on.

The 'Good Chief' in African and European Eyes
But there is a middle range of African political authorities for
whom it is really important to please the colonial government,
although to do so implies a new and often uneasy relationship
with their own subjects. This is another of the many paradoxes
of the imposition of Western values on the non-Western world.
The former colonial powers, whatever may be thought of their
economic motives and policies, have made it their ideal, however inadequately attained in practice, to rule justly in the field
of law enforcement and to secure from their indigenous agents
the same standards that they set themselves. Moreover, they
have sought to introduce into the lives of their colonial subjects
the kind of technical improvement that is expected to make the
people healthier and their agriculture more productive. They
have sought the first aim through the supervision of the chiefs'

judicial activities and the second by inducing them to make and enforce appropriate regulations. To any colonial administrative officer, a 'progressive' chief or 'energetic headman' is one who is tireless in exhorting his people to obey such regulations and not unwilling to prosecute them for failing to do so.

But this image of a good chief is nothing like the traditional image. In the eyes of the African villager chiefs have the right to demand tribute and certain services, and the right to punish disobedient subjects. But they have not the right to demand obedience to whatever commands they may choose to give, and if they try this they may find that their subjects leave them and emigrate to the territory of more easy-going neighbours. As for the headman, *his* image is that of a benevolent senior kinsman who maintains internal peace in the village and does not harass his people with inexplicable commands from higher powers. He is in the difficult situation of all those who are expected to exercise authority over people they live among; the situation is more difficult the more alien are the values of the superior authority.

In Africa this kind of conflict has taken dramatic form in connection with attempts to enforce measures of protection against the erosion of the soil by the traditional methods of cultivation. There are different ways of doing this, but most of them involve building some kind of earthwork to stop the tropical rain from rushing downhill and carrying the topsoil with it. This is the kind of preventive action that is no use unless everybody does it, so it is reasonable to make it compulsory. But it adds to the burden of the farmer's work, the value of it is not always clear to him, and the methods prescribed have not always in fact been technically efficient.

Thus it has come about that soil conservation rules have been seen as the very symbol of alien oppression and the African authorities who enforce them as traitors to their own people—collaborators or, as they are more popularly called, stooges, a word which appears in strange guises in vernacular newspapers.

The New Élites

In this resistance to the new exercise of authority there is another element, and one that has had more influence on the course of history. This is the influence of the new educated class into whose hands political power has passed in one African country after another. The story of their relations with the old authorities of the small-scale societies in which they grew up is a complex one; there have been different phases at the different stages in the conquest of independence.

Education is the key to the world outside the village and chiefdom; this is a truism. It leads to employment in the police, in the courts, in the offices of Native Authorities and those of central governments, in the teaching profession and the Church; and as the generations go by and the attainable level increases, it is the key to the skilled professions. It is the Western-educated who can aspire to play in the new wider society roles more rewarding than those of unskilled labourer and purchaser of enamel pots and pans. It is they also who find that in practice the roles open to them are circumscribed by a political system imposed from outside; and to them this fact is more important than the fact that the wider stage was created, and could only have been created in the space of two or three generations, by the Western rulers with their technical knowledge.

In earlier chapters discussion has been concerned with the new relationships into which people spontaneously enter when they are confronted with new opportunities. In the context of political development, however, we have to consider an additional factor, the limitation of the opportunities which the new situation has seemed to offer. The Western-educated found that they were offered only subordinate roles in the organisations which extended throughout the new wider political units; and where authority within the older ethnic divisions was reserved to members of traditional chiefly houses there was little room for them there either.

This, and not the failure to 'create a sense of nationhood', can be justly debited to the continuance in British territories of the Native Authority system into an era when it no longer had the legitimacy derived from general consensus. Probably most students of politics will agree that no change is ever made at the ideally perfect moment; when a deliberate change is made it is always either premature or long overdue. A government which is not accountable to an electorate is not likely to be predisposed to change in the system it is used to, and any person who is enmeshed in a system is likely, unless he has an exceptionally critical mind, to be well provided with arguments for its maintenance. This, rather than the need for docile tools of oppressive policies, explains the reluctance of British colonial authorities to recognise the inadequacy of most traditional chiefs for the functions of twentieth-century government.

But this is not understood by the young men, and even the not so young men, who find themselves debarred from the seats of power, even the limited power exercised by a Native Authority. As these men learn the various conceptions of democracy that are current in the world, they interpret the maintenance of chiefly authority as a denial of human rights and as deliberately designed for that end. In some African territories the attitude of those Europeans who continue to assert that the chiefs are inherently, and must be forever, the appropriate spokesmen of their people lends colour to this view, since this argument is invoked as a reason for disregarding 'trouble-making politicians'.

So opposition to rule by chiefs comes to be linked with opposition to rule by Europeans, and the early manifestoes of African politicians typically denounce them as agents of imperialism, and corrupt and tyrannical in the exercise of their power. The president of Guinea, M. Sékou Touré, shortly after he assumed office abolished chiefs with a stroke of the pen, but no one else has gone so far.

Chiefs in the New States

In the territories under British rule the policy adopted after the second world war was to democratise the chiefs without abolishing them. First, knowledgeable commoners were added to their councils. Then an elected element was introduced. Eventually chiefs and their traditional councillors were in many places reduced to a minority in elected bodies. Then the chiefs became formal presidents, but withdrew entirely from the conduct of business, in councils that were now modelled on elected local authorities in Britain, but they were still allowed to nominate a proportion of the members from among their own councillors. This in broad outline is the system that was introduced in Ghana and in the Yoruba region of Nigeria before these countries became independent, and other countries were expected gradually to follow their example. The change was made at the same time that the central governments of the territories were made representative.

Where this was done the chiefs lost their formal responsibility for the conduct of public affairs. It is hard to say in a single general statement how much actual responsibility they had exercised as Native Authorities, for this depends, as was suggested earlier, on the kind of administrative organisation at their disposal and on the values which they brought with them to the office of chief. They were all in a position to give orders and have them enforced, but many of them depended for the keeping of records and for correspondence with superior authority on clerks who had had more schooling than they had. These bureaucrats became the servants of the new elected councils which took over the functions of the Native Authorities, and further bureaucrats joined them.

But if chiefs ceased to fill offices that were recognised in the new constitutions they did not cease to exist or to count. It is less easy to follow their activities and to assess their position in the independent states than it was when they were agents of colonial governments, and both their place in the political system and their individual conduct were the subject of periodical reports and endless discussion. But one may venture a few generalisations.

To begin with, Africans do not all react in the same way to the new influences from the Western world. This is a truism; indeed it is in a sense the theme of this book. Some of them seize upon new opportunities; others regret the dislocation of the order they have grown up to take for granted. To these latter the chief is *par excellence* the guardian of the established order; it is they who resent the innovations that chiefs have made at the prompting of colonial rulers, but it is not they who demand the removal of chiefs as 'stooges'. Characteristically they are the rural dwellers who are still in the great majority, and who in much of Africa are still cut off by illiteracy and poor communications from the ideas that circulate in the towns. This is not to say that they do not respond to the nationalist slogan 'Freedom'; but they do not give much thought to its political implications.

For such people the disappearance of the chief is unthinkable, not only on account of his value as a symbol of an established order but because he has ritual functions without which it is supposed that they cannot prosper. In the coastal areas of Ghana, from which that country's most sophisticated population comes, people were complaining a few years ago that the rains were poor because the allowance made to chiefs by the new councils was not enough to provide the necessary ritual paraphernalia.

But the conception of chiefship is valued by more sophisticated persons too. Indeed it might be said that even those who condemn chiefship in the abstract will respect *their own* chiefs, and that this has become easier where chiefs are no longer the scapegoats for unpopular government measures. There are several reasons for this. One is the pride in African culture as the expression of the African personality, which has accompanied the appearance of the new African states on the world stage. The leaders of these new states seek Westernisation with a difference; they are determined to be as good as their former rulers, but equally determined not to be identical with them. We must wait to see whether industrialisation, if it is successfully achieved, will obliterate all traces of political systems based on a simpler technology. In the meantime chiefship has by no means lost significance.

The very people who attacked the Native Authorities, on the two counts that they were agents of imperialism and that they were arbitrary and unprogressive, have been anxious to preserve the institution, and in some ways even to take part in it, as soon as they came into power. Though it is rare for a leading politician to belong to an important chiefly family, several of them have the right to the title of chief, and they generally use this. Even Dr Nkrumah recently succeeded to the chiefship of his home area. The greater the reputation of the politician on the wider stage, the less does such a title add to it; in Dr Nkrumah's case it is his people who are honoured by his becoming their chief. But the significant fact in this context is that he does not seek to assert his advanced views by repudiating such a position as an anachronism.

This recognition of chiefship does not of course imply any wish for the political domination of chiefs. But even the most sophisticated politicians usually wish chiefs to continue to exist, set apart from ordinary folk and treated with particular respect. They define the character of this respect in a different way from the chiefs themselves; to the politicians respect for a chief should not imply asking his guidance on how to vote in elections, while chiefs have no hesitation in giving such guidance. The politicians see the appropriate position of a chief today as something like that of a hereditary monarch, something like that of a hereditary peer.

There is no doubt that today the elected politicians have the upper hand in any serious clash of authority, and they have various ways of making it unrewarding for chiefs to use their local influence in opposition to their policies; for example, by the recognition of a rival candidate in a dispute over succession, or by re-drawing the boundaries of a local authority, since it has nearly everywhere been found necessary to make the lowest level of local authorities correspond with the areas of chiefdoms.

There is an interesting contrast between the constitutional status accorded to chiefs in Nigeria and Ghana. In both countries there must have been a compromise between what chiefs would have liked and what party politicians were prepared to give, but the outcome has been very different. In Nigeria the chiefs have been fitted into a two-chamber system on the Westminster model. In each of the three Regions of the Federation there is a House of Chiefs with amending and delaying powers comparable to those of the House of Lords. The greater *de facto* power of the Emirs in the north is reflected

in the greater voice of the Northern House of Chiefs; whereas
the other two can do no more than delay a measure six months,
the Northern House can press its opposition to a point where
it has to be resolved by a joint session of both Houses. In order
to be eligible for membership of a House of Chiefs a person
must be recognised by the government as being a chief. But
there are far more men so recognised than are admitted to
membership. A few have this right as it were *ex officio*. The rest
are elected by their peers in such a way as to give equal representation to the administrative divisions of each region. Thus,
chiefs are called upon to represent persons who are not their
own subjects; unless it is to be taken that chiefs as such form
an interest group for which any of their number can speak.

Ghana, on the contrary, seeks to keep the chiefs 'out of
politics' while preserving their traditional rights and dignities.
The fundamental provisions of the republican constitution
include the principle 'That chieftaincy should be guaranteed
and preserved'. Chiefs are authorised to do what custom entitles
them to do, including mediating in disputes where not more
than £50 is at stake, and to receive revenue from the land
traditionally attached to their office (though this land is now
managed by elected local authorities). Houses of Chiefs, in
each of the six regions into which Ghana has been divided for
administrative purposes, deal with such matters as disputes
over precedence or succession. All their decisions must have the
approval of the President. Chiefs may not accede to office without his confirmation; he may depose or exile them. In fact they
are subject to a control at least as strict as it was under colonial
rule, though they have lost their administrative responsibilities.

The traditional hierarchy—the chief himself and his hereditary councillors, or those on whom he confers titles of his own
favour—is still the centre of a little world that looks inwards
for the values that it cherishes most. Is this to be explained
simply by the fact that at one time the chief was entrusted
with authority by an alien ruler? I think not. The basic
fact in my opinion is that community of language and culture,
and association with a common territory, *are* the source of the
kind of consciousness which is popularly called 'national' if the

number of people who share it is large, and 'tribal' if the number is small. The divisions of Kenya, where the various African peoples do not recognise chiefs and so the employment of chiefs as agents of policy was out of the question, have been mentioned earlier. The determination of the less numerous among them to retain complete control over the land which has been recognised as theirs, with a view to blocking immigration by more populous neighbours, is an illustration of the same attitude. It is the attitude of people who are more acutely aware of their relations with their nearest neighbours than of any wider field of common interest, and it is bound to characterise those in whose experience these are the only significant relationships.

Micro-Nationalism

But it is the essence of contemporary social change in the political field that these smaller units are incorporated in larger ones in which their members are now expected, at least formally, to play an active part. Whereas the other changes in social relationships described in this book can be analysed in terms of the choices made by individuals when confronted with new opportunities, in the context of politics we have to see individuals as they see themselves, as members of groups with common interests opposed to those of rival groups.

In the days of journeys by foot, of communication by word of mouth, political experience was inevitably confined to relations with immediate neighbours. The widening of political horizons has come from the vicarious experience gained through literacy and the actual experiences of travel to places of education, to places of work, in some cases to fields of battle. The experience of travel for education, or even travel to a secondary school in a distant part of the same territory, is one shared by a small minority, and it is commoner in the west than in other parts of tropical Africa. In West Africa the nationally minded, those who have a conception of the new large-scale state as an entity with common interests, are, in the main, men who have first attended the small number of secondary schools in their own country and then gone overseas for higher education. The present leaders of the new West African states have learnt their political ideas in Lincoln and Howard Universities, in London, in Manchester, in Paris, and have there found common ground with Africans from other parts of their own countries and from other territories altogether. This process is going on all the time; it is paralleled, however, by the creation of associations of students away from home with a common home background, where they can meet, talk in their own language and exchange personal news. In London it is usually students from Nigeria who form these locally based societies. Like everyone else, they see themselves sometimes as members of the narrower and sometimes of the wider group.

Common experience at a place of work has been the most important influence in those parts of Africa where education is less developed. This is an aspect of urbanisation which must be discussed more fully in its place. But here one should mention that political movements in Central Africa have sprung initially from the common interests of unskilled workers rather than from those of the intellectuals of whom there are still so few. And here too one finds that the wider common interest is recognised in some situations, the narrower in others.

The experience of foreign service in war has often been given as a reason for the increase in political consciousness that the post-war world has seen in African territories. It is true that the discontent of returned soldiers has been one element in the demands of Africans for control of their own destinies, notably in Ghana, which led the way in the progress towards independence. But it would be difficult to demonstrate that this was the expression of new conceptions of common interest such as can be clearly seen in the new classes of intellectuals and wage-earners. It is a truism that travel only broadens those minds that have been prepared for broadening.

In the new African states, then, we find 'men of two worlds', not so much in the sense that each man has to accommodate himself to two contradictory worlds, as in the sense that a small minority see political problems in terms of the state as a whole and the world outside it, while the great majority are still pre-occupied with small-scale rivalries within the state. This disparity in outlook accounts for many of the difficulties of the new states in Africa and elsewhere.

It has been an obstacle to the creation of political institutions of the kind that a twentieth-century state is supposed to need. In the British territories representative local government was considered to be such an institution. Among many advantages with which representative local government is credited is the fact that it gives the populations of small areas with common interests a say in the allocation of resources for public purposes. But how small? The smaller the unit the fewer the resources. All local government schemes have adopted some criterion of the minimum population that could make a viable unit, and always this has entailed the combination of groups which had previously thought of themselves as distinct. Almost always the smaller unit has resented the merger, and the resentment has been expressed in terms of traditional political allegiance; 'our chief was always independent of their chief', or 'we will not pay taxes to those people'. The common interest is measured by politics, not by geography.

On a larger scale, this micro-nationalism has led to proposals to divide the present three Regions of the Federation of Nigeria so as to make eight or nine, and to a constitution for Kenya which leaves that country's central government with dangerously little power. In Uganda the rich and populous kingdom of Buganda made good a claim to a federal relationship with the government of Uganda, and instantly its smaller and poorer neighbours demanded the same status, claiming it as the right of any nation with its own ruler. Here another interesting phenomenon was seen; the people of Busoga, who had been divided into a dozen tiny kingdoms, put forward the same claim. Its mouthpiece was the president of the elected council for Busoga which was created under British administration, a man who had no claim to be the ruler of all Busoga, though he belonged to the royal house of one of its bigger kingdoms. This man's family had been pressing the British administration for a long time to recognise his position as hereditary, and the British administration, preferring the elective principle where tradition did not rule this out, had always refused. Nevertheless, he arrived in London in the spring of 1962 along with the three kings of Toro, Bunyoro and Ankole, and negotiated with the Secretary of State for the Colonies on the same terms as they did. What is interesting about him is that none of the separate Soga kingdoms appears to have disputed his pre-eminence; Busoga did have a corporate consciousness.

Clearly a common language and institutions patterned on the same model are factors propitious to the growth of such a consciousness. But they do not always create it, as can be seen among the tiny states in the coastal area of Ghana, which have in common the Akan language, a characteristic political structure and also a system of religious beliefs. This is one of the areas where attempts to combine small chiefdoms in local authorities have met with the strongest resistance.

I do not attempt to offer an explanation of this difference. One reason may lie in the religious functions of the Akan chiefs, which they performed with a conspicuous display of rich regalia that can rightly be described as an expression of civic pride. Yet the Soga kingdoms must also have their communal rituals, though we hear less about them.

This strong sense of community within small political units is an obstacle to the operation of democracy as this word is understood in the part of the world which considers itself to be not only 'democratic' but 'free'. The very notion of representative government, interpreted as it now is to mean that every adult, or at least every male adult, has a voice in choosing his rulers, implies that large populations spread over wide areas can agree on some common interests that they wish these rulers to promote. But in one African country after another it has proved that the only interest that is common to all the inhabitants of a single colony is that which unites them in opposition to the colonial power. When the colony becomes a state its internal divisions appear or reappear. Each section believes that only one of its own members can be an adequate spokesman of its interests. Small units see themselves as permanent minorities condemned to perpetual neglect, and since every unit is a minority of the whole, any one can consider that any given measure discriminates against itself.

Chiefs then have retained their significance as the focus of unity for populations to whom their traditional ethnic solidarity continues to be more important than the new solidarity of nationalism. But the particularism of these groups with common language, culture and tradition, for which English has no word as convenient as *ethnie*, the term used by French writers, and which cannot meaningfully be called tribes—this feeling can exist even without such a focus, and it is a significant factor in the politics of the new African states. It is inimical to the readiness to compromise on which representative government depends. But it is no use deploring small-scale patriotism and thinking people can be lectured out of it; it is there.

Local and national interests become intertwined, so that in those African countries where there are competing political parties the choice between them may be determined by the personal association of a leader with one side in a local context; or a party may win a bridgehead in new territory by supporting a dissatisfied faction there; or it may even build up a following from small political units overshadowed by more powerful neighbours. Many alliances are concerned with competition for traditional offices or titles. They can be illustrated from the rivalry in the Western Region of Nigeria between the Action Group, with its almost exclusively Yoruba membership, and the National Council of Nigerian Citizens with its main support in Ibo country. The existence of these two parties is itself a striking illustration of the importance of ethnic solidarity, though not in this case of loyalty to a chief. Dr Azikiwe founded a party which he envisaged as embracing all Nigeria, though in practice it originally drew its members only from the sophisticated minority in the south. He was joined by Chief (then plain Mr) Obafemi Awolowo, then the leading Yoruba politician, but their alliance did not last long; he accused Awolowo of putting sectional before national interests, Awolowo accused him of aiming at Ibo domination and left to found his own Action Group. The question 'Independence for whom and of whom?' was already implicit in their quarrel.

But people who had some local reason for opposing the friends of Awolowo stayed in the NCNC. In his home town, for example, the successful party in a chiefdom dispute, which had had his assistance, followed him in the breakaway, while the opposing faction kept to their NCNC allegiance.

After representative government had been introduced in Nigeria, for local authorities as well as at the centre, the capital of the Western Region, Ibadan, was the seat of a regional government with an Action Group majority and a town council with an NCNC majority. One reason for the success of the NCNC in the local elections was the hostility between Ibadan and Awolowo's home country of Ijebu, both Yoruba districts.

In the Congo pre-existing 'micro-nationalisms' have been manipulated by external interests; but they were not created by those interests, and the alignment of political parties when elections were held in 1960 was dictated primarily by them. The major opposition was between the parties which wished the Congo to enter on independence with a unitary government and those which looked to a federation with the greatest possible regional autonomy. This is the pattern that has become familiar to everyone following the evolution of the new African states; the peoples who expect to command a majority of seats in a central legislature are for centralisation, the minorities for devolution. In the Congo it was complicated by the nature of their geographical distribution.

The rivalry of longest standing between Congo peoples is that of Luba and Lulua. In the centre of the administrative district of the Kasai province called by the Belgian authorities Lulua, the name of the dominant population, is the city of Luluabourg, which was founded by the German explorer Wissman long before the annexation of the Congo by Belgium. Wissman was on friendly terms with the Lulua. His support enabled one of their chiefs, Kalamba, to establish his authority over a number of previously autonomous Lulua populations, and Kalamba's successors maintained this position. But it was not they who supplied the labour to build Luluabourg. As has happened in so many places, novel forms of employment had no appeal for peasants content with the yield of their own land, but immigrants from farther away responded to these opportunities. These were the Luba, who ever since the days of the

Arab slave trade had been steadily moving northward and westward into Lulua country. Luba built Luluabourg; they provided the labour force for the railway and the Kasai mines, and soon were filling all the posts that called for literacy or mechanical skill in Kasai and many also in Katanga. In addition Luba immigrants took up land in Lulua country to plant cash crops, and about 1925 the Belgian authorities recognised certain areas as belonging to the Luba. Their leaders claim that they are now the largest ethnic group in Kasai province, and in Luluabourg in 1960 there were nearly three times as many Luba as Lulua, so that the election of two Luba mayors is in no way surprising. When the Lulua began to go to school, and to look for employment, it seemed to them that all the good jobs went to Luba; and this gave them a ground for resentment which was aggravated by the resentment that all peasant populations feel towards outsiders who encroach on their land.

This is the kind of situation that develops to a crisis with the introduction of representative government, even, or perhaps especially, representative local government. The possibility that both populations should be represented by persons supporting a common policy is not considered: the only question asked is, which will be on top? for this is the only question that the people's experience prompts them to ask. This is the question that all nations are asking when they put difficulties in the way of naturalisation, but in Africa it is being asked by the component parts of populations which had been expected to accede to independence as single nations.

When political parties began to be formed in preparation for the municipal elections of December 1958, the final step towards representative government in the Congo, the Luba, scattered as they were in different parts of the territory, supported the *Mouvement National Congolais* led by Patrice Lumumba, himself a member of the small Tetela tribe, which aimed at independence with a unitary government. The Lulua accordingly supported the rival *Union National Congolais*, also a non-tribal party which advocated a unitary Congo; since the aims of these two parties were nearly identical the only issues to divide them were local hostilities, and the UNC soon dwindled into a Lulua party interested primarily in opposing the Luba. The MNC success in municipal elections increased the anxiety and resentment of the Lulua.

A confidential government report proposing various means of regulating the status of Luba in Lulua country became public, and was denounced by the Luba as unfair to them. Inflammatory speeches were made and there was fighting between Luba and Lulua. A meeting arranged to bring the two sides together reached an agreement that all Luba in Lulua country who were not actually in employment, numbering 110,000, should return within the next two months to a rural area from which they had earlier emigrated because they did not consider it worth cultivating. The administrative authorities, arguing that a transfer of population could not possibly be made without causing frightful hardships, refused to recognise the agreement. Nevertheless, about 65,000 people did move into areas where no food crops had been planted, and the result was famine. The Luba now demanded the creation of a Luba state in which they would be united with Luba in the neighbouring Katanga province.

In this province too the Luba were an unpopular immigrant minority. Their settlements on the land were in the northern part of the territory. Although they provided much of the industrial labour force, they did not have the near monopoly of the better-paid posts which they enjoyed in Kasai, for the Lunda, the original inhabitants of the mining area, themselves sought these, and as far as possible kept out the Luba, or so the latter thought. In times of recession the Luba labourers were the first to be discharged and sent home. Thus they were predisposed to oppose M. Tshombe as the representative of the Lunda, even apart from his secessionist policy which would have divided the Katanga Luba from those in the Kasai. Accordingly they supported M. Lumumba as the opponent of M. Tshombe. In the Kasai Lumumba's party had both Luba and Lulua members, and a split soon developed between them. M. Albert Kalonji, the Luba leader, formed a breakaway party, which, though it retained the party name, took the opposite line on the only controversial issue, namely whether independent Congo should be a federal or a unitary state. His breach with Lumumba inspired an accretion of Lulua to the Lumumba section. He then allied himself with M. Tshombe, but in so doing forfeited the support of the Katanga Luba, for whom Tshombe as a Lunda was the principal enemy. The opposition of M. Kalonji to the founder of the party to which he originally belonged won for M. Lumumba the support of all the small groups who were afraid of Luba domination.

M. Lumumba's allies in the governing coalition of the first Congo parliament included seven Kasai deputies who joined him simply because he was opposed to, or had been opposed by, the leader of the Luba in the Kasai, *and also* the seven Katanga deputies who were opposed to M. Tshombe, and who included the Luba of the Katanga. The principle 'my enemy's enemy is my friend' had been carried to remarkable lengths.

The 'Erosion of Democracy'
In each of the new states the educated minority which takes the widest view is committed to the operation of a representative constitution under which national policies are implemented by a nation-wide bureaucracy. The English-speaking states entered on independence with constitutions drawn up in consultation with the British Colonial Office. The French-speaking ones made constitutions for themselves which were closely modelled on French examples. Every such constitution provides a set of roles to be filled by actors who are new to them and unfamiliar with the style in which they have traditionally been played.

This is how a student of social relationships describes the situation; a student of political theory might say the new politicians had not learned the conventions according to which certain types of institution are worked, and even that they were unfamiliar with the assumptions implicit in the idea of representative government.

Most observers of the political evolution of the new states are concerned at what has been called the erosion of democracy, without necessarily accepting crude interpretations in terms of the 'unfitness' for it of the peoples who have had no previous experience of it. Some see the explanation of divergences from the ideal of tolerance of opposing views, and its expression in the formal recognition of an opposition party, in the traditional procedures of the small-scale states in which the new politicians grew up. This is thought to be the appropriate explanation for a social anthropologist to give, and there may be some who do give it.

Of course it is true that the highly specialised and not very widely accepted notion of the parliamentary opposition, holding itself in readiness to form an alternative government as soon as it can secure an electoral majority, is not to be found in the traditions of any African polity. Of course it is true that African methods of reaching decisions supply no precedents that could profitably be followed in the government of large-scale states. But some writers tend to assume that the new African leaders are in fact seeking precedents from their own cultural heritage, and that this explains departures from the Westminster model in the new English-speaking states (the Paris model, latest edition, is proving easier to follow by those who have adopted it.)

This is the assumption of those anthropologists who see men as moulded by the culture in which they have grown up so that they can only react to any situation in ways that are already familiar to them. Social psychologists who are closely allied to this school of thought see social change as a process of learning new ways of behaving as one learns a technique; the successors to the colonial government have got the do-it-yourself kit without the rules.

It would be a better metaphor to say that they have been cast for a play in which the *dramatis personae* are enumerated but the lines are not written. The new African governments are recruited from new men, men who never played governmental roles in the long vanished traditional systems or even in the modified versions of these systems maintained under colonial rule. The relationship of the leader with his followers, of ministers with their colleagues, with bureaucrats, with the general public, are new relationships. The leaders of the newly dominant party are likely to be a band of friends who have worked together in the nationalist period when they were deemed subversive, and later in the transition period of collaboration with the outgoing colonial civil servants. It is possible that they may come predominantly from one part of the country, the part where schools have been longest established, and this of course is what gives rise to the association of certain parties with particular tribes, and the fears of their neighbours that government will be carried on purely in the interests of the dominant tribe. But even if this is so, their relationship has been built up, not out of herding cattle or cleaning roads with the young men's companies, but in school, in college, or most important of all overseas, where they were participating continuously in Western institutions.

Of course it is true that the mass of the people, some of whom still have never left the village, and most have never left Africa, have also been assigned parts in the new play without having the lines written. But it is not they who decide whether or not the new constitutions are to be operated with the same conventions as those on which they are modelled.

Interpretations of the 'erosion of democracy' as the result of inability to throw off the shackles of the past are then, I suggest, unconvincing. I would prefer to see it as a further instance of what I have suggested already as the main motive force in the social changes I am describing—the response to new opportunities of individuals who see advantage in them. I do not mean by this that African politicians are in it only for what they can get out of it. I am sure that their ideas of national achievement are sincere, the more so that they have not had time to learn how seldom political ideals are attained. But it is in the pursuit of these ideals that they take the shortest way—the short way with opposition. There are, after all, precedents among the older nations for every infringement of civil liberties that we have seen among the new.

Some critics of the new states talk as if tolerance of political opposition was a moral virtue like industry or thrift, which good men display and thereby show that they are good. Such an attitude ignores the kind of social pressure that is in fact responsible for the practice of the virtues that are cherished in any given society. Good men do not practise thrift in societies where this is equated with meanness, nor industry in circumstances where this would lead to a reduction in piece-rates. Political tolerance has not anywhere been the expression of pure self-restraint on the part of rulers; this is why the price of liberty is eternal vigilance. But in the new states the proportion of the population whose interest in politics goes beyond cheering the leader to thinking about the issues that have to be decided, and wanting to say what they think, is so small that there is no effective pressure for political tolerance. Of course the men in power 'understand' what Western democracies mean by tolerance of opposition views, but they also understand the arguments that can be invoked against such tolerance, and are also invoked in the Western democracies; and they use these arguments when it suits their book. It is certainly not some characteristic of 'African tradition' that is behind their attitudes and actions. It is true that in African languages the word for 'enemy' is often the only one for any opponent. This might be important if the people who carry weight in African politics were the ones who speak only African languages; but they all speak European languages and use their concepts to discuss political matters. If there were to be much talk to popular audiences on the rights of the opposition, the word would be integrated into African languages and people would work out its meaning by using it, as people do with all words.[1]

If 'democratic principles' are not followed in the new African states—and in this context the phrase describes the political procedures of a minority of the states in the world—it is not because no African can understand democracy, but because too few Africans understand large-scale politics. Active participation in politics is of necessity confined to the literate few, even though their position has to be formally legitimised by a popular vote. That those in power seek to stay in power is a truism of politics the world over; they do not do this by wooing the populace away from their rivals unless they are obliged to do so. What obliges them is not intellectual adherence to a set of moral principles, but the co-existence with them of groups of persons organised to defend their interests and claim their

1. A pompous word has already been invented for this: 'phonetic inclusion'

rights. In so far as such organisations have appeared in Africa they did so when it was the colonial governments against whom claims had to be enforced and rights defended, so that when independence came they were close allies of the new rulers, and in most cases were fully incorporated into the dominant party.

Several African politicians have advanced arguments for the inappropriateness in African circumstances of a political system which tolerates competition between parties. One argument, which European writers say they have heard from Africans, is that in traditional African councils dissenting views were given a fair hearing, but the dissentients had to be silent once the decision had been made. This is uncommonly like what we are told of the people's democracies. But it is irrelevant to the circumstances of the new governments because it concerns a different type of discussion. African traditional councils met to take once-for-all executive decisions, not to lay down principles of continuing policy. They did not decide questions by majority vote, but went on talking till agreement was reached, or at least opposition withdrawn. If this did not happen, either no action was taken or the losing side hived off and ceased to participate in a common council with the winners. A section which acquiesced against its will did not try to upset the decision, but it certainly did not forget its dissatisfaction. It is meaningless to try to interpret contemporary deviations from the pure principles of the two-party system as attempts to follow a traditional principle. There is no analogy between a difference of opinion on specific issues and a continuing opposition of views about the lines on which the whole business of the state should be conducted.

So the African politicians do not for the most part hark back to tradition for their justification. They say that opposition cannot be tolerated while the state is in jeopardy from the machinations of neo-colonialists; this is the appeal to the requirements of an emergency, which is familiar in Europe. Some of them also say that there is no need for opposing parties in Africa because there are no opposed classes, and here they are nearer to an explanation of the absence of parties such as are characteristic of 'the West'. There may be individuals who think themselves unjustly treated. But, although there are organisations of farmers, women, youths and so forth, these have usually been created by the dominant party as sections with their appropriate tasks; they do not consist of people with a sense of a common interest that they have to defend. The only such groups are the territorially based ethnic divisions, and they pursue their aims not by opposition on principles of policy but by demands for autonomy which do indeed threaten to disrupt the state.

One can interpret the present-day relations of chiefs with their subjects in terms of the playing of old roles in new circumstances, but this interpretation will not fit the relations of Presidents and Ministers with the people who are now subject to their authority. Nor can these be explained in terms of failure in learning, as some social psychologists try to explain them. The new independent constitutions are not games that a coach could teach them to play in the recognised manner, nor moral systems which would be correctly followed if those in charge of them had mastered the right moral principles. Like the markets for labour and for cash crops, they have created new situations offering opportunities to those who know how to take them; the wage-labourer, the cash farmer, have their new roles defined for them by the expectations of the employer or buyer, and have to accommodate these with the expectations attached to their traditional roles. The new rulers have their roles defined only by the constitution, and there is no society in which this is sufficient definition. Most of their subjects have no specific expectations from them; no norm that they should not transgress has won general acceptance, and so there is no support within the new states for the few politically sophisticated men who know that the right of opposition is recognised in some older countries and seek to claim it for themselves.

CHAPTER 5

NEW TOWNSMEN

Growth of urban concentrations—The modern city—'Detribalisation'—West African towns—Central African towns—New types of association—Division and realignment among overseas Chinese—Conservative townsmen—Women in town.

As NEW TECHNIQUES have made it possible to develop the resources of tropical countries, urban concentrations of population have grown up on a scale not known before. Of course the life of cities did not begin with the industrial revolution. Archaeologists regard the building of cities as the beginning of civilisation, and social anthropologists distinguish between small-scale societies that are wholly autonomous (which some call 'primitive' though others prefer to avoid a word with derogatory associations) and 'peasant' societies in which the village is dependent upon the town as a centre of administration where justice is done and taxes collected, and perhaps also as a market for its produce. Such a relationship of the village and the town was characteristic of pre-industrial India, China and Japan as it was of medieval Europe. The town itself has been defined sometimes by the characteristic that its inhabitants do not get their subsistence directly from the land, but by exchange for the products of specialised crafts or from incomes which they receive in payment for services; in other words, the existence of towns depends upon, as it promotes, a commercial economy. Others would define a town merely in terms of the concentration of population. Unless it has a wall round it, or unless it is part of a political system in which areas of authority are strictly defined, it is difficult to decide who shall be counted as part of the town population. Where colonial governments make themselves responsible for maintaining urban standards of building and sanitation, for providing roads and water supplies, an area with quite a small population may be treated as a town; usually one where a few Europeans, government servants and businessmen, and a few shopkeepers (in Africa often Asians and in Asia often immigrant Chinese) are gathered round an administrative station. Handbooks enumerate, for whatever country they describe, the number of its towns which exceed a certain population. One of the diacritic figures is 100,000. Nearly all the towns in Africa which exceed this figure are centres of industry or commerce created by European entrepreneurs. But the empires on the southern fringe of the Sahara had their smaller walled cities to which merchants came from as far away as the Mediterranean coast, and some of these, such as Timbuktu, have a history going back over many centuries. Some West African coastal towns, too, grew up in the eighteenth century as entrepôts for a trade with Europeans —largely in slaves—in which Africans were the middlemen.

The life of most of the dwellers in such towns was not, and still is not today, as sharply distinguished from life in the countryside as is that of the town-dweller in an urban civilisation. Unless transport and resources are sufficient for whole urban populations to live on food brought from great distances, a large proportion of them must still be farmers cultivating fields as near as they can get them to where they live. Many of the inhabitants of Ibadan and other Yoruba towns have one town house and another house on a farm, where they live for part of the year. This has made it difficult sometimes to induce them to pay rates for urban amenities.

The combination of urban and rural features was characteristic of these older towns before the colonial era. The town was then a governmental capital, and the home both of numerous craftsmen of various kinds who supplied the court and exchanged their wares in the market, and also of even more numerous farmers whose life was just what it would be if they lived in a concentration of houses too small to be thought of as a town; some of the craftsmen might themselves be also farmers, or at least other members of their families were. Ibadan has grown in the last decades because it has been made the capital of the Western Region of Nigeria, and this has drawn to it politicians and civil servants and labourers to build and maintain assembly halls, offices, houses and a university; and also because individuals who have made money as cocoa brokers or transport contractors or lawyers, or just as cocoa farmers when prices were high, have chosen to invest their wealth in town houses. Ibadan has its millionaire's row. It is the home of a Yoruba society stratified on new principles. But it is still a Yoruba town.

The Modern City
In marked contrast are the cities that have grown up where nothing was before, in centres of industry created by Western capital and techniques, particularly where minerals are worked, as on the central African copper belt or on the Rand, or at ports and railway termini. Here the framework within which social relationships are carried on is imposed by an authority alien to the mass of the population, that of governments and employers in varying combinations.

Whereas in Ibadan and many other West African towns the bulk of the inhabitants are ethnically homogeneous, and are on their home ground, the much larger populations of these new cities are of diverse origin and have all originally come there as strangers from home areas more or less distant. This generalisation applies as much to most of the non-African as to the African populations, though for the purpose of this study it is the changes in the societies to whom industry is a new way of life that are significant.

The entry into new social relationships which I have described as the essence of social change obviously covers a wider field of experience for a greater number of people in the towns than it does in the rural areas. I have suggested that, as industrialisation proceeds and migration from country to city becomes cumulative, it must be in the cities that the institutions of a large-scale African society will be built up. It is in the cities that people become aware of new common interests, and form associations to pursue them which, for some purposes at least, transcend the ethnic cleavages that play so large a part in the politics of the new nations. It is in the towns that the educated find employment, that they can get together and formulate political demands and programmes and that they can readily gather and influence large audiences.

The re-ordering of social relationships in the new urban populations is largely spontaneous, as any such re-ordering must be, but it is necessarily affected by the extent to which their lives are regulated by superior authority, and this is necessarily greater in towns than in the country. The time they spend in wage employment is wholly organised by outsiders to any society to which they consider themselves to belong, persons with values and expectations quite different from those of the village. The process of adjustment to the new circumstances—the making of townsmen, as it has been called —may be significantly affected by the aims of the governing authorities. This is so particularly in those African cities where it has been the policy of Europeans in political control to regulate the immigration of Africans and limit the numbers who may make their permanent homes in the cities.

But it is not only the obstacles created by authority that make it difficult for a peasant to become a townsman. It is an over-simplification to argue, from the obvious attraction of the towns as places where a better income can be earned than is usually obtainable elsewhere, to the conclusion that inside every peasant there is a townsman struggling to get free. This is to disregard the great number of readjustments that the peasant must make in his life if he is to commit himself to dependence on wage-labour. People do not readily uproot themselves from the place where they feel they belong if there is something there that *belongs to them*; and the something, in African conditions, is their right to a share of lineage land. It has been remarked that the labour supply for the expanding industries of the industrial revolution in England consisted largely of men who already, as farm-hands, were wholly dependent on wages; and a study of factory workers in Puerto Rico produced the interesting result that of 291 who had come from work on farms, all but nine had been landless labourers. Asked if they would like to go back to agricultural work, 60 per cent replied 'On no account' and 25 percent said they would do so only if they had land of their own. Thus, it is not merely the difference in mode of life that leads some townsmen to keep one foot in the country.[1]

The African labourer is not a proletarian. Often his land does not give him a living, certainly not in terms of his cash requirements, but it is there; it is his security—

> 'the place where, when you have to go there,
> They have to take you in.'

'Detribalisation'

It was customary once to describe African town-dwellers as 'detribalised'. The word had associations rather than a precise meaning, and in the main the associations were derogatory. It implied the existence of a 'tribal' order of society which, for Africans at least, was the desirable state. Detachment from this, it was considered, resulted in that absence of sanctioned norms that Durkheim called *anomie*; or, since few of those who use the word had read Durkheim, that 'tribal' Africans were honest and obedient to authority while 'detribalised' ones were corner boys. Opposing this view the liberal South African, Professor W. M. Macmillan, took the line that 'detribalisation' was a process of social evolution which all the industrialised nations must have gone through and which Africans should be encouraged to go through in their turn.

Other writers have rejected the word as meaningless; the process of industrialisation, they hold, is a continuous one, and there is no precise point at which a person can be held to have become detribalised.

Of course there are, in all the big cities of central and southern Africa, Africans who have been born and grown up there and have no effective links with the village from which their forbears came; yet it may still be that they prefer, at any rate for

1. Peter Gregory, 'The Labour Market in Puerto Rico' in W. E. Moore and A. S. Feldman, *Labour Commitment and Social Change in Developing Areas*, 1960, p. 144

some purposes, to associate with people whose ethnic origin is the same as their own. Are they detribalised?

The concept owes something to the notion of 'culture' as the field in which the student looked for change. In this frame of reference detribalisation might be measured by the type of furniture in a house or the type of worry which leads people to consult a diviner. If, however, one is thinking in terms of the maintenance of social relationships, one will ask first what is the relative strength of a person's ties with his neighbours in town and his friends and kinsmen in the country. As long as he is moving to and fro between these two environments, he will be subject alternately to different social pressures, that of his immediate associates being stronger at any given moment, but not so much so that the obligations belonging to the other context are entirely forgotten. This is the situation in which Gluckman[1] has said that the migrant labourer is 'detribalised' in town and 'de-urbanised' every time he goes home again.

At the time when wage labour was a novelty, the social pressures of village life, and particularly the obligations of seasonal work in the fields, weighed heavily on the labourers; they tried to dovetail this with work in the towns, and if they were obliged to enter into contracts which made this impossible, they did their share of ploughing or clearing the ground at any rate in the year in which they went away. But as time went on they came to see the goods and wages that they brought or sent home as their contribution to the village economy, and their time in the village as more like a holiday. After this there was less reason to come home often, and the periods of absence in town grew longer and longer. But people could not regard the town as their home unless they married and set up house there. This was not always easy. Even where it was not municipal policy to limit immigration, it was as hard to get a house as it is for the lowest wage-earners in most expanding cities. But it is not only this kind of obstacle that keeps many Africans with one foot in the country; it is also their strong attachment to the

---

1. 'Anthropological Problems arising from the African Industrial Revolution', in Southall, ed., *Social Change in Modern Africa*, 1961, p. 70

place that they can think of as theirs as no one else's. It is pertinent here to note that the Ghanaian farmers who have moved into the cocoa belt and made money there often invest their profits in a large house in their home area. Something must be said later about people who while in town deliberately maintain the values and the social relationships characteristic of their rural homes. But the main theme of this chapter is the development of the new social relationships that life in town makes both possible and necessary.

West African Towns

Newcomers to any strange city will, if they can, seek out someone who is already known to them to help them find their way about, or, in default of personal connections, someone who at any rate speaks their language. Most Western cities have their concentrations of immigrants in particular localities; not to give more hackneyed examples, I lived for fifteen years in London between a 'Polish corridor' and a 'Kangaroo alley'. As the immigrants find their way about, they begin to merge more and more with the general population, provided that no obstacle is put in their way; in an American or western European city the next generation reveal their origin in little but their name. Perhaps the most important factor in this assimilation is a uniform system of school education, which all children have to go through.

The independent West African cities set aside areas at a little distance from the main town—outside the walls, if there were walls—for foreign traders to live, and in the great centres of trade there were separate quarters for different peoples. These persist today in the Zongo quarters of the Ghanaian towns, and even more conspicuously in the 'stranger cities' outside the capitals of the Northern Nigerian Emirates. There, today's immigrant population consists more and more of the large numbers of southerners who are employed as clerks in the elaborate administrative systems of the Emirates, organisations that call for educated employees in numbers greater than the North can supply, and in the railway, post office, banks and European trading firms. The immigrants from the South are in a different position from those in the industrial cities; indeed their situation has points in common with that of the European residents of a past generation in Turkey or China, or Chinese residents in Siam, though they have not had the political power to demand special privileges. They are despised as infidels by the Orthodox Muslim subjects of the Emirs, while they see themselves as representatives of a more advanced civilisation, and make this clear in their dealings with the man in the street; and they are in fact indispensable agents of economic development and so have been brought in in ever greater numbers as development plans have been launched. Since they are for the most part employees and not independent traders, southerners in Northern Nigeria do not seek economic protection; but they resent their exclusion from political power.

The relation of the immigrants with the northerners reflects in an acute form the deepest cleavage in Nigeria—the opposition between the conservative North, which dominates the federal government by virtue of its numbers, and the up-and-coming Eastern and Western Regions. At the time when Nigeria began to move towards independence, the southerners were pressing for the early withdrawal of British rule while the North, fearing that for them British personnel would have to be replaced by southerners, was more hesitant. This conflict of opinion was of interest only to the educated minority, but its expression in the form of abuse of Northern rulers as imperialist stooges was something that anybody could understand, and it kindled latent prejudice into an active hostility that was dramatically expressed in 1953 in three days' rioting in Kano. The 'stranger' population of Kano live in two 'satellite towns' close to one another and to the walls of the ancient city. The smaller, the Fagge, is the traditional dwelling of 'stranger' Hausa. The larger, the Sabon Gari, is a modern township built to accommodate the more recent influx of southern immigrants. Its population trebled in the fifteen years from 1939. There is no formal segregation of northerners from southerners, but the former are 97 per cent of the Fagge population and the latter 97 per cent of the Sabon Gari. Thus there is little opportunity for proximity to have a 'mixing' effect.

In May 1953, when the Northern Emirs had been publicly abused in Lagos for obstructing Nigeria's advance to self-government and a virulent press campaign was being waged against them in the South, the Yoruba political party, the Action Group, proposed to hold a meeting in the Sabon Gari. When it seemed likely that northerners would try to break it up, permission to hold the meeting was cancelled; this news was broadcast, along with a message from the Emir asking northerners to keep out of the Sabon Gari. Nevertheless, a crowd did collect outside the place where the meeting was to have been held. Presently a southerner rode by on a bicycle; the crowd attacked him and smashed his bicycle. This was the signal for attacks on all southerners and counter-attacks by southerners on northerners. Fighting went on through the next two days. Rumours spread that northerners living in the Sabon Gari were being systematically slaughtered. Both sides were seeking revenge for actual or imagined injuries, but, as the anonymous author of an official report puts it, the northerners came to see themselves as engaged in a preventive war.[1] (This did not prevent individual northerners in Fagge from sheltering and protecting southerners living there.)

In such circumstances the concentration of people in towns does not iron out their differences but rather accentuates them, and indeed this is equally true of the relations between the European and African populations in the industrial centres. To some extent the consciousness of common interests tends there to break down ethnic antagonisms, but in so far as it does so it is only in relations between Africans, the great majority of whom form a single economic class. In the cities of Northern Nigeria the indigenous and the immigrant African populations do not have common economic interests, though it may be that common opposition to the political values of the North and its general way of life is creating a sense of unity among southerners who would be antagonists on their home ground.

These cities are divided by the kind of conflict that in the West would probably be called 'racial'. But their immigrant in-

1. Northern Regional Government, *Report on the Kano Disturbances*, 1953, p. 39

habitants have thrown in their lot with the city; they are not constantly looking over their shoulders at a rural home to which they periodically return. This is partly because many of them come from densely populated, overcrowded areas, but also, and perhaps mainly, because they have a secure livelihood in town.

Central African Towns

In the great industrial centres the African immigrants are in a different situation. They are by every reckoning the least sophisticated members of the population, and even where it is not official policy to treat them as sojourners, there are deterrent influences at least as strong as the incentives to throw in their lot with the city. They arrive unfitted for any but unskilled labour, and they may often be prevented by legal or trade union restrictions from rising any higher. Where the limits to the advancement that can be achieved by sticking to one job are so low, people readily move from one employer to another and one town to another even if they do not go back to the country.

Yet it is here, if anywhere, that that sense of common interest which is needed to make new states into new nations could begin to be felt.

Studies that have been made by social anthropologists in the Copperbelt towns of Northern Rhodesia show how the immigrants from different home areas sometimes align themselves as tribes in opposition to traditional enemies, sometimes classify strangers by tribal affiliation and ascribe stereotyped characteristics to them on this basis, and sometimes combine to pursue common interests to which tribal origins are irrelevant.

People with the same home background would be expected to cluster together in a foreign city, though the modern city authorities do not seek to group them together; indeed anyone who wants municipal housing has to take whatever is going. But other circumstances too may cause members of particular tribes to claim a particular status or to be associated with a particular kind of work. Thus on the Copperbelt there are differences between the peoples who have had members working there since the mines were opened and those who have more

recently entered the labour market; and differences in the
length of time that schooling has been within their reach also
affect the status that people from different rural areas can
expect to attain. Both these differences are matters of historical
accident. On the Copperbelt both factors have favoured the
various peoples from Nyasaland, who in the cities are always
called collectively Nyasas, though at home they are divided
between the inhabitants of a dozen different areas speaking
different dialects or even languages. Missionaries were at work
in Nyasaland much earlier than they were in Northern
Rhodesia, and their pupils were in demand as clerks in the
Copperbelt towns when there were no literate men anywhere
nearer. Nyasaland had also provided a large part of the labour
force for the older mines in Southern Rhodesia, and by the time
the copper mines were in full production they were used to
underground work and were preferred to completely in-
experienced labourers from the nearer neighbourhood. Later,
as the peoples of Northern Rhodesia began to offer themselves
for this work, Nyasalanders were made their instructors. As the
numbers of mine employees increased, and more and more
peoples were represented among them, the Nyasalanders came
to be a minority, but they retained a prestige as a result of which
they have provided many of the leaders and spokesmen of the
whole labouring population. Their claims to leadership are
sometimes contested by the Bemba, who now form the majority,
and who, strong in their traditions of past conquests, maintain a firm belief in their inherent superiority over others. The
Lozi, who also fill a high proportion of clerical posts, and who,
like the Bemba, have an aristocratic tradition of dominance
over their neighbours, also compete for pre-eminence with the
Nyasalanders.

The latest comers, the hicks who don't know their way
around, are always at the bottom of the prestige scale, and in
the conditions of an African city they are apt to be differenti-
ated from the rest for a reason mentioned earlier—that when
men are new to wage-labour they go alone to the towns leaving
their families at home. Hence they live together in bachelor
quarters and are not mixed up with neighbours from other

home areas. On the Copperbelt this is the position of the Nyakyusa from western Tanganyika, who before the second world war rarely left their homes to earn wages, but who are now the largest single group after the Bemba.

The only people who will take the job of removing night-soil are the Luvale speakers from the far north-west, on the Angola border. Whatever the reason for this, it leads the other peoples to despise them.

Thus, a 'tribal' or local name (for obviously 'Nyasa' is not the name of a tribe, and names which are those of tribes are often used by outsiders to apply indiscriminately to a famous tribe and all its neighbours) calls up in the minds of those who use it prestige, or the lack of it, and perhaps other stereotyped associations. It gives to anybody moving to and fro in the shifting populations of the Copperbelt towns a rough guide to what he can expect of an otherwise unknown person.

How far is a common tribal name, a common home, a common language a basis for the ordering of social relationships among tribesmen? It is clear that it can hardly be so unless there is more interaction between people who share these attributes than between them and others who do not, and this can hardly be the case if they are regularly mixed up with others in work-gangs in the daytime and as neighbours in the evening.

Epstein,[1] working in Luanshya and the Roan Antelope mine township, observed that the mine authorities had been led astray by assuming that, if men in town recognised tribal membership, they necessarily also brought with them the whole structure of relationships characteristic of rural life. On this assumption they sought to establish lines of communication with the employers through representatives elected from among their number by all the principal tribes, and called Tribal Elders. Men who were generally respected were chosen for this office. People referred to them disputes which they were willing to settle by conciliation, and the Elders made these cases the occasion for affirming the norms of good neighbourliness which are not in fact a matter of any particular tribal tradition—

1. A. L. Epstein, *Politics in an Urban African Community*, 1958

though this is how people like to think of them—but a general characteristic of small-scale society. In this way the Tribal Elders kept the peace much as the village headmen did in the rural area.

For a time they were the mouthpieces to the management of complaints brought them by their tribesmen. But when the attempt was made to use them as the official spokesmen of the employees in collective bargaining, it became clear that in this field a mine worker did not wish to be represented necessarily by someone of his own tribe, and did not wish to be represented by anybody whose qualification depended on the values of the rural society. When strikes and disturbances broke out on the mines the Elders could exercise no influence at all; rioters would not listen to them, and strikers accused them of selling out to the management. In the first serious strike, the District Commissioner had to ask the men to name their own spokesmen, and a committee was formed which was able to restrain the strikers from violence; unfortunately there is no record of the way in which it was chosen and who were the members.

When councils were set up to represent African opinion to the municipal authorities, they were at first nominated from among the Tribal Elders. But it gradually became evident that new leaders were arising who did not owe their position primarily to tribal membership, or at all to tribal values. This leadership took the not unfamiliar form of a Welfare Society drawing its membership from the western-educated section of the population—clerks, teachers, clergymen, hospital orderlies —and founded originally by a missionary. It is significant that business was conducted in English. This society made its own representations to the authorities and sometimes persuaded them to take action; although some of those in authority said— as is always said of an educated minority—that they represented nobody but themselves. Others remarked that they showed more initiative than the officially recognised councils, which were apt to wait for a lead from the District Commissioner. It came to be the Welfare Society and not the appropriate Tribal Elder who formally welcomed distinguished visitors from the rural areas—even though these were mostly chiefs.

The first move away from representation on a purely tribal basis was made when the Tribal Elders, authorised to elect representatives to councils to advise the municipal authorities, made the choice not entirely from among their own number but partly from young and better educated men who were prominent in the Welfare Societies. These were men whose common interest in amenities for urban residents—and also in the treatment of labourers, a matter which they made it their business to be interested in—outweighed their attachment to particular tribes and indeed had no bearing on it. A more dramatic development was the rise of industrial organisations which successfully challenged the right of the Tribal Representatives, as they had come to be called, to speak for them *at all*. This was the point when the common interest of workers was formally recognised as more significant for the organisation of an urban population than their separate ethnic origins. Now the African Mine Workers' Union spoke for the mass of the workers in relation to management, and the African National Congress, formed out of a federation of all the Welfare Societies, became the political voice of the African population as a whole in relation to the government. At the same time there grew up numerous other trade unions and associations of people with common economic interests.

This surely must be the way in which wider interests than those of the single tribe come to be recognised. Such a result can only come about where there *are* common interests, those which are experienced in common work and common residence. It cannot be created, or at any rate not maintained for long, by exhortations to 'put nation before tribe'. It is significant too that the consciousness of common interests has arisen where these had to be pursued by making demands of authority; it flourishes, that is to say, on opposition, like the national feeling discussed in the previous chapter.

Every study that is made of new, or rapidly growing, urban populations has something to say about the associations that grow up to meet the needs of the new situations in which the immigrants find themselves. For some purposes they do combine on ethnic lines. The many burial societies which operate in Southern Rhodesia are all confined to single tribes. Mitchell has noted the contrast with Northern Rhodesia, where tribal associations of this kind, though they exist, are apt to be ephemeral and are often no more than drinking clubs; he suggests that the formal recognition of Tribal Elders, though it proved to be unsatisfactory as a link between labour and management, did meet a need for the assertion of tribal feelings in other contexts.

New Types of Association

The Belgian authorities in the Congo, who maintained a close control over the activities of African populations in the towns, required all associations to apply for registration, stating their aims and conditions of membership. A survey of these in Stanleyville gives a good idea of the purposes for which the new townsmen organise themselves in continuing groups. Most of them seem to have originated as 'friendly societies' building up by contributions a fund that members can draw on in sickness, for burials, for journeys home or for heavy expenses of a more enjoyable kind such as feasts; in Africa as elsewhere, a feast for the mourners is a part of all funeral rites. A member of one such association, for women only, said in an interview: 'When somebody comes out of prison, we give them 100 francs and one or two bottles of beer.'[1] Some continue with this as their main object, others combine it with some more specialised interest, and sometimes the specialised interest comes to be the only one. In any such association it is to be expected that the members will be in some sense of like mind, and what is of interest for the student of social relationships is the kind of people who are expected to be of like mind.

The basis of community may be the place of origin, and this may imply an area much smaller than a tribe; it may be a common occupation, as in the associations of houseboys and of

1. P. Clément, 'Social Patterns of Urban Life,' in UNESCO, *Social Implications of Industrialisation and Urbanisation in Africa South of the Sahara,* 1956, p. 484

postal workers (bodies which differ from trade unions in that their aim is mutual aid but not bargaining with employers); or merely common status, as in those of ex-soldiers and of pensioners. Then there are associations of former pupils of various schools, who have in common memories of school routine and of teachers, as well as religious affiliation, since all these schools were managed under the Belgians by Catholic orders. But what is more significant to them is the common bond of literacy; one of these associations provides in its rules that former pupils of other schools may be admitted to join it. Most interesting of the Stanleyville organisations is the *Association des Evolués,* of which Patrice Lumumba was president. This is a counterpart of the Native Welfare Societies on the Copperbelt, but, perhaps because of the strict control of political activity by the Belgian authorities, the aims with which it was registered were not the furtherance of African interests or of the influence of the educated class, but mutual support in the maintenance of civilised standards. Members were required to be monogamous, of blameless conduct, to be engaged in a respectable trade, and to 'stand out from among their fellows in behaviour and general morals'. These principles were held to make manual workers admissible as members. On the other hand, most of the association's activities—the organisation of study groups, choral singing, dramatic performances and sport—were focused on interests that could only have been developed at school.

In this self-selection of a 'civilised' élite some observers see the beginning of a class system which should eventually become more important than the ethnic divisions that characterise the world of small-scale societies, and obstruct the development of political units of larger scale. But this is not necessarily what the Africans themselves want, as witness their argument that there is no need for competing political parties where there is no conflict of classes. The South African writer, Mr Ezekiel Mpahlele, has remarked on the contrast between the West African states, where there is a great gulf between the Westernised minority and the mass of the people, and his own country where the ceiling on African economic and social mobility keeps 'the enlightened and the unenlightened' much closer together; indeed modern wages policies offer higher rewards to semi-skilled labourers than to intellectuals[1] (some would say this is true of Western countries too).

M. Clément remarks that the Stanleyville associations with tribal membership do bridge this gulf, in so far as educated men join them and usually become leaders in them, and this is true too of the speech-group associations of overseas Chinese which will be described later. Comments such as those of Mr Mpahlele and M. Clément imply a preference for different values from those which I have assumed in considering the city as a melting-pot. Which is to be preferred? The ideal of the equalitarian society and that of the unified nation are equally treasured by many Western thinkers. The latter has in practice proved easier to attain. For the new large-scale societies the alternative seems to be the maintenance of 'vertical' divisions, between persons for whom a common origin is more important than the differences of wealth and status among them, and 'horizontal' divisions in which the common interests that go with membership of social class transcend the differences born of diverse origin. Unity and classlessness do not seem to be mutually compatible. If neither can be attained by deliberate effort, the choice is no more than a choice of private Utopia.

One of the most interesting organisations mentioned by M. Clément is based solely on residence in the same street. Its members are the oldest inhabitants, and so are well known to one another. It is fundamentally a drinking club, and in this respect like hundreds of informal groups who expect to meet for a drink at the end of the day's work, but it also organises Christmas celebrations, and its members contribute to the cost of funeral rites in one another's families. Its speciality, however, is its mode of procedure. It makes great use of written communication, even to next door neighbours; it imposes fines on its members for incorrect behaviour (for example, if a wife interrupts the gathering) and it gives its members titles which belong to offices in the government (governor, district commissioner, etc).

In this respect this organisation resembles one on the

1. *The African Image*, 1962, p. 62

Copperbelt that has been analysed in much greater detail by Professor Mitchell:[1] the *Kalela* dance team. The *Kalela* is one of many dances performed in emulation by the different ethnic groups represented in the industrial populations of Southern Africa. But it is not a 'tribal' dance if by this is meant a traditional dance from the home area (as some of them are). It is not the property of any one group and it is of recent origin. It is by far the most popular dance on the Copperbelt. Its history is traced back to dances imitating military parades which some say were known in Tanganyika in German days. The characteristics of these were that the leader was called the Governor, all the dancers had military rank, and, as an African who remembered them put it, 'everyone wore good clothes'. The name *Kalela* means 'pride', and the teams who dance it compete with one another.

As the *Kalela* is performed nowadays, the dancers wear European clothes and not African finery, and each team includes some named officials, though no longer military officers. The officials do not dance but look on. There is a 'king', who is elected by the members to be their organiser and treasurer, a 'doctor' and a 'nursing sister'—a woman, the only woman member of the team.

As Mitchell points out, although the *Kalela* is not a 'tribal' dance, it *is* a tribal dance. Each team draws its members from one tribe, often from one chiefdom. The attraction of the dance for spectators is not the movement, which is a sort of shuffle, but the songs which are composed and sung by the leader, and these consist mainly in praise of the team and its own people and lampoons at the expense of other tribes. The songs are assertions of tribal solidarity, while the titles of the officials and the immaculate European dress of the dancers symbolise the way of life of the dominant class in the urban society and the prestige attaching to those who are able to follow it. The *Kalela* dancers are usually young men employed at the lower levels of wages, which do not enable them to adopt Western ways to any great extent. Yet their imitation of the dance is a recognition of a new prestige system, based on occupation and level of income.

1. *The Kalela dance*, Rhodes-Livingstone Paper 27, 1956

All these examples show how African immigrants in the industrial centres see themselves sometimes as townsmen with common interests given by their situation as tenants, employees, educated men or disenfranchised persons, and sometimes as exiled countrymen with a common homeland. Epstein's study of industrial relations shows how wage-earners no longer wish to deal with their employers, nor citizens (in so far as they are so) with the municipal authorities, through the medium of men chosen for their tribal status, or even elected as their spokesmen by voters grouped according to tribe. Yet it does not follow that in the new associations built around common interests, tribal solidarity has ceased to have any importance. Internal rivalries in such organisations often divide the members on tribal lines. For example, although the African Mineworkers' Trade Union was created to further the interests of mineworkers as a group, when its officers were elected what happened was, as an African commentator put it, that 'each tribe decided that it must have one of its own people as chairman'. When the General Workers' Union failed to get higher wages for labourers, Bemba members complained of the failings of Nyasa leadership. When the higher grade workers broke away from the Mineworkers' Union to form a staff association, one motive was the resentment of the Lozi and Nyasa minorities at what they saw as domination by the Bemba majority, while the Bemba in turn resented and wanted to break the Lozi and Nyasa monopoly of higher level jobs. At one time the Nyakyusa talked of breaking away to form their own union, with some justification in the fact that they had no kin to help them with support when they were called out on strike, and no source of food from gardens of their own as married men had; but they were persuaded against this by an appeal to workers' solidarity.

So one must conclude that in the new comprehensive structure that industrial conditions impose, new forms of organisation have developed that cut across ethnic divisions, yet these divisions are by no means obliterated.

Division and Realignment among Overseas Chinese
Among the newly industrialised—or barely industrialised—

countries Africa has attracted most attention from writers considering these divisions and realignments as an aspect of changing social structures. But similar divisions and realignments have also been analysed among the emigrant Chinese populations in South East Asia. The name given to these divisions by a recent writer, Dr G. W. Skinner, is 'speech groups'. They have been called tribes, but Dr Skinner, in his study of Siam, rejects this word on the ground that it is inaccurate both in the technical and the popular sense.[1] In my view the word has long ceased to have a technical meaning, though there seem to be contexts where one is driven to use it. But the significant differences between the 'speech groups' of Nanyang Chinese are just the same differences that divide African newcomers to cities: language and place of origin. A single speech group in China comprises many million people where the corresponding unit in Africa may number only a few hundred thousand, but the phenomenon of the juxtaposition of different groups in centres of immigration is the same.

Another difference between the Chinese and the African examples, however, is in the length of time during which the process of migration has been going on, and an even more important one is that Chinese immigrants supplied the capital as well as the labour for the industrialisation of Siam. The first street that was built outside the walls of the royal city of Bangkok housed Chinese traders comparable with the dwellers in the early stranger cities of Kano and Timbuktu. It was built at least as long as 200 years ago, and Chinese were settling in Siam long before that, some of them as refugees from the Manchu conquest in 1645. But when Western technology reached South China in the form of steamships, the increase in the rate of migration was sufficient to bring it within the subject of this book. Moreover, the magnet that attracted this flow of migrants was the demand for labour for the development of new industries in Siam.

Five speech groups were represented among the migrants, and have been as far back as there are records of Chinese emigration to Siam. Different groups have preponderated at

1. G. W. Skinner, *Chinese Society in Thailand*, 1957, p. 35

different times in various occupations and localities. The social mobility of the nineteenth-century period of rapid development mixed them up to some extent, and the Japanese occupation and the disabilities that Thailand's nationalist policies impose upon them have driven them to close their ranks; yet the division into speech groups persists.

All five groups come from the Fukien and Kwangtung provinces: Cantonese, Hokkiens (from the hinterland of Amoy), Teochius (from Swatow), Hakkas (from the interior of Kwangtung), and Hainanese from the north-east coast of Hainan Island. The coastal populations first made their way there as traders, and when in the seventeenth century the Thai king made oversea trading a royal monopoly, he employed Chinese merchants and seamen who had skills and experience beyond any of his own subjects; moreover, most of the Chinese ports at that time were closed to all but Chinese traders. Those who settled in Thailand at this time were mainly Cantonese and Hokkiens, the latter in the majority. They lived on the coasts and by the navigable rivers, and in Bangkok itself they came greatly to outnumber the Thai population, which still consisted entirely of courtiers. Some of them were appointed to official positions, ranging from the fairly low level of tax collector to that of governor of a province. Men in such positions of authority naturally encouraged further immigration of their own speech groups.

The most important of these men was Taksin, son of a Teochiu father and a Thai mother, who was actually king of Thailand for fifteen years, and during that time appointed to the governorship of Songkhla, in South Siam, a Hokkien, Wu Yang, who was succeeded in the post by eight other members of his family. The influence of these 'Chinese rajahs' accounts for the large Hokkien immigration into South Siam. But even more significant was the Teochiu immigration to Bangkok, which Taksin made the capital of the country. This brought many Teochius into contact with the Thai officials responsible for managing the royal monopoly of trade, in which they shared; the ships they bought were built and manned by Teochius and sailed to Swatow and the neighbouring ports. Once settled in

Siam they introduced sugar cultivation, and started plantations of it and other export crops.

The first effect of contact with Western technology was felt when Hong Kong became a colony, and a port for ships travelling farther than the Chinese junks could go. Now the Chinese monopoly of trade with Siam was broken, but at first the more significant change was that Cantonese had long-distance shipping lines on their doorstep and could easily go farther afield. From that time on they generally neglected Siam for the lands of greater opportunity under Western governments. Those who remained there, or went on coming there, specialised as artisans and, as time went on, as mechanics, and so were concentrated in the towns. They built the first steam-driven saw mills.

The deliberate modernisation of Siam was set on foot by King Mongkut, who came to the throne in 1851. He abolished the State monopoly of trade, and made treaties with Western nations of the same kind that the Chinese were making at the time. Swatow became a treaty port (open to foreign trade) in 1858, and the steamers that King Mongkut had built for him carried goods there and brought back migrants from its hinter-land—Teochius and Hakkas.

Hainanese meantime had been penetrating farther inland than any other immigrants. They had to travel in junks during the long period when the ports on their island were closed to foreign shipping, and their small junks would take them just as far as Bangkok. They were regarded as lower class by other Chinese. Avoiding the big towns where the others were concentrated, they pushed inland up the rivers. Theirs were the skills of a coastal people, fishing and boatbuilding. They were also experienced in sawing timber, and as long as this had to be done by hand they had a monopoly of exploitation of the teak forests.

All the skills that have been mentioned up to now are those of a non-mechanised society. With machine techniques comes the same demand for labour that created the Copperbelt towns. The labour was required in Thailand for the development of communications—canals, roads and railways. The Cantonese provided skilled workmen; the unskilled were the newest immigrants, Teochius and Hakkas.

Like every rapidly developing country, Siam has been a land of opportunity, and there have been no conventional restrictions on social mobility such as have prevented Africans on the Copperbelt from rising beyond semi-skilled labour. Yet there is still some distinction of status between the speech groups, which can be measured by the prestige of the occupations in which different groups preponderate. A group as a whole derives its prestige from its members of high status. Thus, both Teochius and Hainanese are specialists in occupations of low status, but Teochius are also strongly represented in finance and large-scale commerce. Hokkiens too specialise in high status occupations.

Here, then, no structure of classes with common occupational interests has obliterated the association of different groups each with its own place of origin, which is preserved in the daily use of the different languages.

But although some Chinese immigrants in Thailand attained to high rank and political power and many to considerable wealth, as a people the Chinese were alien immigrants and as such had to build up associations for protection and mutual aid.

For a long time these were confined to single speech groups or even sections of a speech group. The earliest associations (the Chinese name for them, Kong-si, means simply 'company') were craft guilds which succeeded in monopolising their specialities for the speech group that brought them to the country; the activity may account for such curious facts as that in present-day Bangkok, where there are many Chinese silversmiths, nine out of ten of those who make bowls and belts are Hakkas. When the Thai government in the nineteenth century decided to find a source of revenue in the organisation of gambling and the sale of opium and spirits, matters which interest Chinese but not Thais, they farmed out the collection of the taxes to Chinese. These monopolies were the object of fierce competition between the leaders of Kongsis, who organised their followers to terrorise rival bidders; such activities could only accentuate the divisions between speech groups. In the present century the tax-farming monopolies were abolished and the illegal activities of the Kongsis brought under control; some ceased to exist, others became mutual aid societies.

To a large extent, however, this function was now performed by the speech group associations. These had somewhat similar interests to those of the earlier Kongsis, though their membership was wider. The former were limited to single speech groups because they organised specialised crafts practised in particular areas of south China. The latter undertook to look after all interests of members of the speech group, including not only the protection of craft monopolies but help in finding employment and general assistance; they built temples for the worship of the special gods of the home area, and cemeteries for the burial of those who could not be sent home to China as was the ideal. They later began to provide for their members schools giving education of Western type.

In the first decade of this century two organisations were formed which were open to all Chinese—a hospital and a chamber of commerce. The latter became the mouthpiece of Chinese interests in general in dealings with the Thai government. In both these organisations the speech groups maintained their separate identity; the constitution of the hospital provided that the chairman should come from each of the speech groups in turn, and it quickly became a convention of the chamber of commerce that the groups should be represented in proportion to their numbers in the total membership.

These facts can perhaps be taken to epitomise the present relationships of Chinese speech groups in Thailand. Just as Africans on the Copperbelt act sometimes as members of different and rival groups and sometimes as one group in relation to their non-African rulers and employers, Chinese in Thailand, without forgetting their membership of different speech groups, have become aware of common interests as Chinese in a country where they are aliens. This awareness is a reaction in part to deliberate measures by the Thai government designed to limit their place in the Thai economy, and in part to such external events as the rise of nationalism in China (before as well as after the Communist victory) and the deliberate creation of a national Chinese language. One can see parallels here with the influence of African nationalism and the use of English as a common language for African politics in Rhodesia.

On the Copperbelt a sharp class division coincides with the division between Europeans and Africans. In Thailand there is no such economic dividing line between Thais and Chinese, and there are signs that the lowest paid labourers merge in some situations into a class with common interests; yet divisions within them would be likely to follow ethnic lines. This situation closely resembles the relationship between tribes among Copperbelt labourers.

These examples illustrate what is a fact of general experience—that in the large-scale political units of today people rarely forget completely their different places of origin, and always think of themselves as being in some sense closer to others with whom they have this in common, but that other common interests may override these differences. The question of political importance is whether the differences are so strongly felt as to make impossible that minimum degree of mutual tolerance that is indispensable between fellow citizens in a single state. Up to a point they can be recognised by dividing states; but the advantages of Western technology cannot be fully enjoyed by very small political units in territories of limited natural resources. This is why the question what factors can promote the necessary mutual tolerance is of practical importance. It is clear that it cannot grow up among people who are never in contact, nor among people who are in contact only in situations of rivalry. The co-operation of wage earners and people with common professional interests, and the juxtaposition of neighbours in the life of cities, are the most favourable factors, but it is naïve to suppose that they will quickly, or perhaps ever, have the effect of a mint turning out coins all stamped with the same image.

Conservative Townsmen

There are, moreover, people who strenuously resist integration into the urban community and what they hold to be the contamination of urban ways, and this although life in town as wage earners is an indispensable part of their existence. This attitude has been found among a section of the Xhosa in the urban population of East London in South Africa. It stems from the same small-scale nationalism that has been discussed in other contexts, though here this feeling is not, as in the circumstances of South Africa it could not be, expressed in political demands.

The Xhosa have a longer history of contact with Europeans than have most African peoples, and much of it is a history of armed conflict. In each of the succession of Kaffir wars the government of the Cape Colony pushed its authority further. Missions had been established in the no-man's-land, and their converts did not join in resistance to the British; in this century their intransigent fellows would have called them collaborators. The division between collaborators and resisters subsists to this day in the form of a recognised division between the 'School' people, who are at least nominal church adherents, send their children to school, and adopt European ways as far as this is materially possible, and the 'Red' people, who wear the old fashioned red blanket (itself an imported substitute for skins) and rub their bodies with ochre, and who are devoted to the maintenance of the rural way of life that 'the ancestors' would wish to see maintained. Even in the rural areas these sections hold aloof from one another, and in town their aims are different. Both are earning wages in town because they cannot subsist without them. But whereas School people may spend any surplus that they earn on such amenities as the town offers, and on the Western style clothing which has become a status-symbol in so many of the new African cities, Red people devote it to one purpose only—to establish a homestead in the rural area and build, equip and stock it with cattle and sheep. Red people see themselves as possessed of those pristine virtues that romanticists for so many centuries have associated with rural life.

Their form of nationalism is not that which seeks to take over control of the way of life of the alien rulers, but that which repudiates it altogether. To them treason is not confined to those who act as the agents of government policy, but is the action of everyone who in his personal life willingly departs from the standards set by his tradition. This idea may not be clearly formulated, but what is clear is that people who seek to follow 'civilised ways', and go to work in town as a means to this end, are on 'the other side' of a dividing line that was drawn a century and a half ago.

In modern conditions it is impossible for any Xhosa to make a living from his holding of land. Under the present policy of the South African government it is also difficult for Africans to establish themselves permanently in town. But whereas many School people would probably become townsmen if it were not for these difficulties, the Red people have no wish to do so.

In their own eyes they are honest, law-abiding, thrifty, careful how they bring up children to respect and obey their elders; while townsmen, and those who fall for the temptations of town, are liars and thieves, learn all kinds of vices from what they see at the 'bioscope', do not keep their children in order and waste their money on frivolous amusements. School people in town may have the same stereotyped picture of the vices of town life, which, of course, they too deplore, but they see the Red people as uncouth, dirty, unsophisticated and ill-mannered.

Nevertheless, the two sections are mixed as neighbours and workmates, just as are the different tribes on the Copperbelt or the Rand. But the Red people have consciously, and to a large extent successfully, resisted any external influences that might result from such juxtaposition. How they do this is the theme of Dr Philip Mayer's recent study of East London.[1]

Every newcomer to town seeks friends from home to help him find his way around. But a Red Xhosa in East London seeks to associate solely with other Reds from his own home area all through his working life. 'Home people' are primarily those from a single headman's area; the concept may extend to include those from neighbouring locations. Newcomers to town live as 'boarders' sharing a room with someone else from home;

1. P. Mayer, *Townsmen or Tribesmen*, 1961

as soon as he can, a man rents a room of his own in which he can choose who will be his 'boarders'. This will usually be his permanent home as long as he is working in town, and it will seldom be far from the room where he started his urban life. Since the Xhosa wage-earners do not go home for periods of more than a few days, there is much more continuity in the urban population than is characteristic of the Rhodesian towns. At the same time, they are expected to go home at every break in work which is long enough to give them time for the journey.

Red Xhosa form groups of half a dozen who meet to drink and chat at the end of the day's work. The sharing of beer is itself the traditional expression of hospitality and friendship, and the purpose of these gatherings is, as they put it, to 'talk about home. Home news and thoughts of home as far as possible occupy all their leisure hours. Traditional etiquette is followed, with much solemn discussion of breaches, and of the fines to be paid by the offender (in the provision of more beer).

In Xhosa tradition men who have been initiated together are expected to be linked by close bonds, and in the towns these age-sets of young men form clubs which meet every Saturday night. Each has its recognised leader, and acts as a tribunal to settle disputes between its members (as does the drinking club).

Some occasions call for a meeting of all 'home people', notably the death or serious illness of one of them, or the commission of an offence by one member against another; as far as possible, Red Xhosa in town deal themselves in the traditional manner with breaches of the rules that they recognise, and do not let them go before a magistrate. These meetings are the close counterpart of the village moot at home. The only sanction behind their decisions is to ostracise the recalcitrant member; and if he is one of those who find Red traditions irksome and wants to 'abscond', as the Reds put it, if he has already found a footing in the wider society of the town, this is no sanction. But all these groups with their recognised leaders and their periodic meetings do help to hold the Reds together as a closed community and to keep their values alive, including the value of obedience to elders.

Other forces operate to the same end. All Red Xhosa in

town are expected to go home as often as they can, and when they are there they bring news with them. The sanctions of 'gossip and scandal', the fear of the disapproval of those whose opinion is valued, are nearly as effective as if they were still living in the homestead. Then, the way is not easy for them to enter the groups which break down the divisions of rural life. All the associations which do so—churches, sports clubs and the like—represent the values of School people; not only should they be repudiated by the good Red, but his lack of sophistication would embarrass him should he try to join them; this is true even of the churches.

Yet Reds do 'abscond' and become townsmen, either learning to read in night-school or adopting less demanding 'School ways', or simply rejecting the company of 'home people' and the sanctions that go with it. The city has always been the place where those who are impatient with the rules of a narrow community can escape from them, and what is remarkable about the Red Xhosa is the degree of success with which they have prevented this. A most important factor in this is the practice of sending home those children who are born in town; not only because of the evil influences to be encountered in town, but because it is thought right for a child to be brought up in the typical rural homestead with the grandparents at its head, and there to learn respect for seniority, and what the life is like for the sake of which they in their turn will have to go to town to earn and save.

The sending of children home is not peculiar to the Red Xhosa; it is characteristic of many African wage-labourers. But because the Red Xhosa reject Western values with such determination it has the effect among them of producing generation after generation of wage-earners who refuse to become townsmen.

The Red Xhosa, then, are perhaps the only remaining Africans who go to town solely because necessity drives them and not at all for the sake of opportunities that the country does not offer. Yet even among them there are some who see the town as a place of escape. Youths with this aim cut themselves off from the 'home people' as soon as they get to town; if they fail to make their way in town, outside observers as well as the Xhosa will call them irresponsible; if they succeed, the Xhosa will call them 'absconders' and outside observers will call them enterprising.

For these youths the Xhosa way of life implies a long period of hard work, self-denial and subordination to their seniors, which they can see is not imposed on other townsmen. At the end of it, however, they can look forward, if this appeals to them, to returning to the homestead which their earnings have founded and living as respected elders, whose sons in turn will go to town and work to maintain the Xhosa way of life.

Women in Town

But others living in Xhosa society have to endure irksome subordination with little or no prospect of winning through to a position of respected authority. These are the women, and particularly the School women, who on the one hand are not allowed to join in the country amusements that are allowed to Red girls, and on the other are conscious of wants, notably for clothes, that cannot be satisfied without an independent income. Older women have additional reasons for going to town. Widows cannot support themselves in these days when the rural homestead must have a wage-earner to keep it going. The same is true of women whose husbands have 'absconded' and no longer support them. Then there are unmarried mothers, who by Xhosa custom, which differs in this from that of many African peoples, are unmarriageable.

In town a woman who finds a job and keeps it has money at her own disposal and is not, as she is in the country, a perpetual minor. She has, in fact, achieved the essential aims of all feminist movements. She has also, of course, flouted the rules of her own society, as all feminists have done. What is most disturbing to many observers of city life in Africa is that most urban women find sexual partners who do not marry them, since most men in town are earning wages to support wives in the country, and many women are women who are disqualified from marriage. This is what is often called the promiscuity of urban life.

Of course there are more opportunities for casual sexual relationships in town, and it is easier there for the fathers of casual children to disown them. But this should not be taken to imply that all sex relations are promiscuous or that all children are neglected and grow up delinquent, still less that all the women who go to town go there to make an easy living through casual liaisons with men. On the contrary, an unmarried woman who goes to town not only wants to, but has to, have her own independent earnings. She expects to have the main financial responsibility for her children.

Young people may go through a series of short-lived affairs, but as they get older they prefer a more stable relationship. What offends in these relationships is not that they are promiscuous, but that they are not sanctioned by the rules either of School or of Red people. In the eyes of School people they lack the one recognised legitimation, that of marriage. In those of Red people a sexual union between a married man and an unmarriageable women is permissible, but a domestic union is impossible without marriage. Yet the most stable of these partnerships are those in which the partners share a dwelling and the co-operation in daily affairs characteristic of husband and wife. Women do not break up these relationships; they do not willingly flout the Xhosa principle that all a woman's children should have one father. Women as earners have an independence that they could never have in the country, but they do not often take advantage of it to abandon their partners; more often they seek to detach the partner from his legal wife at home.

By Xhosa standards, and indeed by the standards of all societies which are opposed to easy divorce, the man should resist this, and should not seek to treat his town children in the same way as those of his legal wife. Their mother and their mother's people are responsible for them as they would be in the country, and many of them are in fact sent home to the mother's people, and are therefore no more neglected than the children born in town of married parents.

It is the contention of this book that the changes that non-Western societies are going through, though they were imposed on them at the outset, are now essential for the realisation of aims that they have made their own. In terms of individual actions the process can be seen as one of response to new opportunities, which include freedom to choose one's way of life and dispose of one's own earnings. Women, as well as men, seek this freedom, in the non-Western as in the Western world. In the Western world too this is still deplored by many people. But most Westerners would now at least give lip service to the emancipation of women, with whatever mental reservations. It is worth remembering that this is one aspect of the migration of Xhosa women to town and their life when they get there. Most of the new towns present the dilemma that is already familiar to the West, of the readjustment of family life to fit a new conception of the status of women; it is hardly for Westerners to deplore the fact that this readjustment is being attempted.[1]

Xhosa townswomen, then, are much more whole-heartedly committed to the city than Xhosa men; to them the element of choice in entering city life is much more important than that of necessity. It is their way, and their only way, of escape from the status of perpetual minors. It is not an easy way; it is a gain to be allowed to stand on their own feet, but it may sometimes be a hardship to have to, the more so as Xhosa women, like many others, want, if they can, to combine independence with a congenial sexual and domestic union.

1. I am myself among those who have written about urban *anomie* where tribal restraints are inoperative and nothing takes their place. Recent research has shown that, although the tropical cities have their share, and perhaps more, of the social problems characteristic of urban slums, the picture is not so black. There *is* a public opinion and there *are* common norms of conduct. More important, the social problems must be solved *in the towns*; these exist, and must inevitably grow, as the poorer countries turn to industrialisation as the solution of other equally pressing problems.

CHAPTER 6

NEW RELIGIONS

Religion in small-scale societies—Witchcraft—The response to missionary teaching—Secular repercussions of mission teaching—Millenary religions—The cargo cults—African Messiahs—Other independent African Churches—Magicians and 'witch-finders.'

MOST PEOPLE BELIEVE that human affairs are in some way dependent on forces more powerful than humanity. In common parlance these are generally called supernatural, but some authors who have written about small-scale societies reject the word on the ground that the people described do not see these forces as being outside nature, and they prefer some such term as 'ultra-human'. A distinction that has a longer history in the discussion of such beliefs is that between religion and magic. Notably the name of Sir James Frazer is associated with the idea that man advanced from a stage in which he believed that he could manipulate natural forces by means of magic to one in which he understood that he must appeal to a divine power, and so religion came into being. There is certainly a popular notion that beliefs and practices which can be called magical are morally and intellectually inferior to those which can be called religious, a notion appropriate in societies where a church lays down a body of doctrine, but additional ideas are current about the contact between men and ultra-human forces, which the official doctrine does not countenance. Rationalist students of society, such as Durkheim, have also distinguished between religion and magic and treated the former as morally superior. Malinowski saw both as manifestations of the same human need for reassurance in the face of forces that man cannot control;

he was interested in asking why such beliefs and practices could be seen in some form in every society.

Malinowski too distinguished magic from religion, but on quite different grounds from Durkheim's. For Durkheim magic, to which he gave very little attention, was essentially anti-social, whereas religion reinforced social order through public ceremonies. Malinowski believed that both magic and religion had social functions, but that magic was concerned with specific aims whereas a religious rite was an end in itself. Most people would agree to call collective ceremonies religious; but if individually performed rites are to be called magical, what are we to say about private prayer? Certainly it is true that, as scientific knowledge increases man's control over nature, religion comes to be concerned more with moral values and less with appeals for divine intervention in human affairs; even so, Christian public rituals include many specific petitions. Anthropologists recognise today that, although one can describe a ritual in common-sense terms as predominantly religious or predominantly magical, no criteria can be found for a sharp division into separate categories. Some think it better to use the word magico-religious for the whole complex of activities, based on beliefs about the nature of ultra-human forces, that seek to regulate man's relationship with them.

Religion in Small-scale Societies

What is important for societies of simple technology is that such beliefs generally present a picture of the world as a moral order, in which rules of conduct have ultra-human sanction and prosperity should follow right dealing. Of course they are confronted, as was the writer of the Book of Job, with the fact that sometimes this is patently not so, but every system of beliefs has some answer for this difficulty.

Typically the world is believed to be peopled by spirits on whose good-will man depends, in the sense that any kind of misfortune may be ascribed to the loss of it. In addition there is often a class of actions that are thought to bring down automatic retribution in the form of sickness, without the intervention of any personified being; such actions usually include sexual transgressions, but the same kind of ritual punishment is sometimes believed to follow involuntary acts or contacts that have no moral significance. This range of possible sources of punishment in the form of sickness or other misfortune is also, it should be noted, a range of possible explananations and hence of possible means of putting right what has gone wrong. Of course these explanations cannot in fact solve the problems for which they are invoked, but they can relieve the sufferer of the burden of suffering without hope of remedy. Christian missionaries have sometimes asserted that people who hold these beliefs live in perpetual fear of malevolent powers. This is not the interpretation accepted by anthropologists, whether Christian believers or not, who have lived among them.

Every people has its own pantheon, and though they may believe in a creator god who made the whole world they do not think they must force their neighbours to worship the same one as they do. Indeed, although it has been reported from Africa that the creator god is the main object of the worship of the Nilotic peoples, many others pay little attention to him and direct their ritual to the spirits of their own ancestors. If they are politically organised under a chief, his ancestors may be held to interest themselves in the well-being of the whole people, and in this case he will approach them in national rituals; or there may be other national gods for the upkeep of whose priests and temples he is responsible. Such religions are in their essence particularistic, 'national' if you like; the objects of their cult are tied to specific descent groups or localities and they could not exist outside these limited contexts.

Rituals which are performed on behalf of all the people, and at least ideally attended by them all, do serve to affirm their unity, whether through a rule that quarrels must be reconciled before the national feast, or through dramatic performances such as that of the Zulu first-fruits ceremony representing the triumph of the chief over his enemies. Their overt purpose is to thank the ancestors for the harvest and beg their blessing for the future on people, cattle and crops. One might think of these recurrent rituals as keeping the world on its normal course.

Others are needed in case of disaster. Public disasters such as drought and epidemics are likely to be explained by failure to maintain the public cults, or perhaps in modern times by some departure from custom that displeases the human mouthpieces of the ancestral spirits. They call for public ritual at appropriate places. But what is perhaps more interesting, and is certainly less generally understood, is the ideology which explains private misfortunes. It is characteristic of the religion of small-scale societies that many kinds of personal misfortune are believed to be caused by personified beings. When a man is sick or a woman barren, the appropriate specialist is called upon to find the cause by divination and recommend appropriate action. In Africa this might be thought of as the main field of magical activity, though it is very different from the typical magic of the Trobriands as described by Malinowski. There certain specialists secretly utter magical spells over the gardens and the canoes to make them prosper; the magician there has a public function similar to that of the Zulu chief appealing to his ancestors, or the priest of the earth goddess in Ibo country. This illustrates yet again the difficulty of drawing a clear line between religion and magic.

The African diviner must find out what action of his patient has given what person or spirit cause to be angry, or brought automatic retribution into play; hence every consultation is an examination of somebody's conscience, and also a public discussion of his and others' actions, in which the question whether the visitation was or was not deserved is crucial. People are always consulting diviners, and these discussions and the further talk to which they give rise make an important contribution to the maintenance of social norms. There will always be some cases where the victim will maintain that he is in the right; what he did was justified in his own eyes, and it may even be that his neighbours cannot see that he has done anything to deserve his sufferings. For such a situation—the problem of evil in its simplest form—African religion has an answer in the belief in witchcraft. Somewhere or other are people who harm their neighbours out of sheer malice; they are witches.

Witchcraft

This is the essence of the belief in witchcraft wherever it is found, and to a student of society it is far more important to understand this than to trace to religions now obsolete specific details of the picture of the witch that has been imagined in particular societies. In seventeenth-century England they rode on broomsticks; in one part of twentieth-century Tanganyika they fly in the form of (invisible) pythons. They are the same at both times and in both places—the personified cause of unjust suffering inflicted on the innocent. Seventeenth-century England would have had to have an official belief in witches if it had not come by that time to have an official belief in the Devil. It is harder to explain the absence of a belief in witchcraft than its presence.

The details of African beliefs about witches—what it is that makes them witches, how their malevolent power operates, how you can know that they are about, or have been—vary from place to place. Many people can tell you what witches look like and how they behave; the 'image' of a witch is of a disagreeable, unneighbourly person, always suspecting slights. People who constantly think someone is bewitching them are usually thought by others to be witches themselves (witches are of both sexes); just as people who think everybody hates them are usually prone to hate others. In some places people are openly accused of witchcraft, in some they are merely talked about behind their backs; in others, people ascribe their misfortunes to anonymous witches but rarely name anyone.

What is most interesting is the type of belief that regards witchcraft as the unjustified invocation of the same powers that may on occasion be justly invoked. This is how the Lugbara of south-western Uganda see the field of ultra-human sanctions for conduct. Certain persons, the elders of lineages, have the right to call down the wrath of the ancestors on people who treat them with disrespect or who cause dissension within the lineage. They do this not by a formal invocation, but simply by thinking angry thoughts, which lead the ancestors to be angry in turn and send sickness to the offender. The anger of the ancestors is described by the same word as the anger of a witch, by definition a person with no right to call down misfortune upon others. In this society with autonomous lineages and no formal judicial institutions, the authority of a lineage head derives from the fact that he alone can approach the ancestors with regular worship, or with sacrifices on behalf of individual members who are found to have offended them. When such a man is getting old his authority may be challenged by the head of a sub-division of the lineage, who is seeking to make his own branch autonomous. The challenge takes the form of claiming the independent right to consult a diviner and perform the sacrifice which he recommends. Dr J. Middleton,[1] the anthropologist who has lived among the Lugbara, witnessed a prolonged contest of this kind. At one point in it a boy fell sick. It was agreed on all sides that his sickness had been caused by the old man whose authority was questioned. But whereas this old man asserted that he was using the anger of the ancestors to punish disrespect, his rival said he had bewitched the boy; the same act, then, was interpreted in both these ways. If the old man was still the recognised head of the lineage, he had justly caused the sickness; if his remoter kin had become independent of his authority, he was an outsider, therefore one with no right to cause sickness, therefore a witch. This is a most striking instance of that possibility of alternative interpretations which makes the system watertight, and provides an explanation of every case to suit the points of view of all the persons concerned.

Among the Nyakyusa, where the witches are believed to fly through the air on invisible pythons, good men are believed to combat them, also flying on invisible pythons. Both are believed to have the same kind of power, and this power may be legitimately used against people who have offended public opinion. The Nyakyusa believe that 'the breath of men', the wind of whispers of disapproval, sets it in motion against an offender. Hence there can always be two explanations of sickness; either the sufferer is an innocent victim of witchcraft, as he himself and his friends will probably believe, or he is being deservedly punished for wrong-doing.

1. *Lugbara Religion*, 1960

The Response to Missionary Teaching

In Africa and the Pacific the extension of European political power was accompanied, and even sometimes preceded, by the activities of Christian missionaries, exponents of a religion which they offered as the only true one for all peoples of the world. They had some striking initial successes where chiefs were converted and made Christianity their official religion; public rituals were suppressed and the mythology associated with them forgotten, and sometimes the objects or images used in these ceremonies were destroyed.

As the missionaries would themselves have admitted, these conversions were not primarily an expression of intellectual or perhaps even of moral conviction. If a missionary was judged to be a good man, and gained influence as a result, the judgment was made in terms of the existing scheme of values; he was good if he was a friend and a bringer of benefits. The missionaries' god may have been similarly judged by existing values and found to be more powerful than the local gods and spirits. More sophisticated interpretations of Christianity had to wait for a later generation, and in some places for more sophisticated missionaries, and, as happens with any religion, the sophisticated interpretations were always those of an instructed minority.

The first missionaries in Tahiti were popularly judged by what their prayers seemed to have contributed to the well-being of the island. 'They generally laugh,' one of them wrote in his journal, 'ridicule and tell us that they have heard before and still are not saved, but continue dying.'[1] Applying the same judgment in the contrary sense, the Samoan who introduced the first missionary to his country asked, 'Can the religion of these wonderful *papalangi*s [white men] be anything but wise and good?' and gave as his reason their elaborate clothing 'and then look at their axes, their scissors and their other property, how rich they are!'[2] A letter from Livingstone records the comment of an African after some experience of mission teaching: 'To be plain with you, we should like you much

1. Quoted by W. P. Morrell, *Britain in the Pacific Islands*, p. 37, 1960
2. Williams, *Narrative of Missionary Enterprises*, quoted *ibid.*, p. 59

better if you traded with us and then went away, without forever boring us by preaching that word of God of yours.'[1]

Indeed, even in the early days of the nineteenth century
when the missionaries were operating outside the range of
British political protection, they were identified with the power
of Europeans in general—their great ships, their firearms and
their many other devices. Certainly to some, probably to many,
of their converts this technical equipment was thought of as the
gift of a god more powerful than any of theirs, and a gift for
which the islanders would qualify if they followed the appropriate ritual and moral prescriptions. This is not to deny the
moral appeal of such concepts as brotherly love, which is not
in fact alien to the values of non-Christian peoples. But when
a chief adopted Christianity and required his subjects to follow
him, he was apt to be motivated by calculation of the relative
power and efficacy of his own and the Christian god. Thus
Pomare, the chief of Tahiti, asked for Christian baptism after an
enemy had defeated him in a battle. When he won a victory in
the next encounter both his enemies and his allies from neighbouring islands became Christian. In Southern Africa, where
missionaries were working among people with more knowledge
of European activities, they were welcomed because they taught
reading and because they could advise the chiefs how to conduct their relations with other Europeans.

The description which Schapera has given of the effects of
the introduction of Christianity to the Tswana could be paralleled in many other parts of the world. He shows that it has
had wide repercussions in the secular sphere, and thus has influenced the lives of many more people than the minority who
are church adherents, and most of whom are as sincere
Christians as would be found in any congregation.

Where Christianity was thus made an official religion, chiefs
exercised their authority to suppress practices of which
missionaries disapproved, among converts and others alike.
Thus Tswana chiefs forbade beer drinking, the payment of
bridewealth and initiation ceremonies, punished their subjects
for working on Sundays, and used their right to call upon the

1. D. Chamberlin, ed., *Some Letters from Livingstone*, 1940, p. 205

labour of their subjects to conscript them for the building of churches.

Polynesians had temples and cult objects burnt; they prohibited polygamy, and also dancing and tattooing, as 'heathen practices'. In Tahiti the chief complained that all laws were being disregarded by people who maintained that they had lapsed along with the old religion, and the missionaries found themselves obliged to draw up a new code, and followed this up with the creation of an annual legislative assembly; and they drew up codes of laws with penalties in various of the islands. These laws then applied to the whole population, whether baptised Christians or not.

In practice the acceptance by pagan populations of new religions thus imposed upon them was rarely unanimous, and religious divisions had political significance where, as with the Tswana, rivals for power could draw support sometimes from people who resented the suppression of traditional customs and sometimes from people who thought it did not go far enough. Kgama, the chief of the Ngwato, illustrates both these attitudes. He was baptised in his father's lifetime, staunchly refused to take part in tribal ceremonies, and eventually rebelled against his father and drove him out. As chief he was uncompromising in forbidding 'heathen' customs, but when he was threatened with the secession of many of his subjects he withdrew his prohibition on beer drinking.[1]

According to Schapera, the rivals of a chief can still make capital out of promising to re-introduce forbidden customs. It is an ironical comment on Kgama's efforts that the proportion of Christians among the Ngwato is the lowest in any Tswana tribe.

In Bechuanaland political difficulties arose also when a chief sought to control the church as he controlled all other activities in his domain, or when persons of high rank or royal lineage who had become church officials supported the local missionary in censuring the personal conduct of a chief.

1. I. Schapera, 'Christianity and the Tswana', *Journal of the Royal Anthropological Institute*, 1958, Vol. I, p. 6

Secular Repercussions of Mission Teaching

The influence of Christian missions has extended over a field far wider than that of church membership because for so long, and in so many parts of the world, they alone provided all the schooling, and hence the only entry to the new opportunities of the commercial economy and the institutions that it brought with it. All the colonial powers except France have relied on Christian missions to lay the foundations of literary education, and in the territories of these powers there was for a long time no other educational agency. It has not usually been practicable for the missions to give free education except at the most rudimentary level, and even when parents are not asked to pay for their children's education they have to provide pencils and exercise books (or slates) and to dress their children more neatly than would be necessary for herding cattle or playing in the village. Thus the school, which is the way to a higher income, is also the place for children whose parents earn more than the average; when secondary education is in question, the ability to pay for it may be a characteristic of a new social class.

Mission teaching, perhaps inevitably, has interpreted the Christian way of life in terms of the missionary's home environment; and of course missionaries are not the only Europeans overseas who judge the advance of Africans in civilisation in terms of their approximation to the externals of European culture. But to make such an approximation requires a cash income—in most countries an income well above the African average. The Protestant ethic, Max Weber would have said, entails striving to earn such an income; but I doubt whether there has been much difference between Catholic and Protestant missions in their emphasis on earning and the improvement of standards of housing and dress. In saying this I am not seeking to romanticise the African hut with the goats tethered to the centre post and the smoke of the fire escaping through the thatch, but merely to show how in some places church membership has come to be thought appropriate for persons earning higher incomes, and how in some places a higher income is necessary for those who wish to live up to the standards of church membership.

This differentiation has not everywhere been equally marked. In Bechuanaland, according to Schapera, there are no external marks of distinction between Christians and pagans. They associate freely in daily life and attend each other's ceremonies; the important distinction is in the restrictions on conduct which church membership imposes, and it is not by externals that one tells how well these are observed.

From Southern Africa, however, comes the most striking account of a sharp differentiation between Christians and pagans: the division between 'Red' and 'School' people in the African areas of the Cape that has been discussed in relation to their respective attitudes towards city life. What is interesting here is the moral superiority with which each section looks down upon the other. The difference here is less in attainable income than in preferences in expenditure; the 'School' people value the external evidence of a 'civilised' way of living, while the 'Red' people prefer to spend the minimum on clothes and house furnishings and save their money to build and stock homesteads in the country.

There are many local differences in the extent to which Christians and non-Christians form separate communities. In the immediate neighbourhood of a mission station there is usually a village populated entirely by church members, particularly if the church owns the land and can decide who is to live on it. The policy of the Catholic missionaries in the Belgian Congo was to require their converts to move away from their pagan homes and join new Christian villages. When, as in this case, the mission does not have the backing of the African authority, there may be another type of political conflict. The Congo missions were accused of encouraging converts to defy their chiefs. The mission is inevitably thought of as a refuge for individuals on whom traditional rules bear hard, especially the marriage rules which many Christian missions condemn. Girls may escape to the mission from marriages arranged for them with husbands they do not like; in so doing they are resisting the authority of their fathers and sometimes also of chiefs. In terms of the mission's values they must be succoured and supported. Hence arise conflicts of jurisdiction which remain unresolved if the field is one in which the administration is neutral.

Millenary Religions

These changes could be called the secular repercussions of mission teaching. But almost everywhere the impact of the Western world has been followed by the appearance of new religious movements led by prophets who claimed direct revelation. Some of these have expressly repudiated the religion taught by missionaries, and with it all the innovations brought by colonial rulers. But the majority have sought to remodel the missionary religion in a form more consonant with the values and aspirations of the prophet and his followers. Messianic beliefs are characteristic of this latter type of cult, but the prophet is often thought to be himself the saviour, sometimes claiming to be Jesus Christ but sometimes repudiating a messiah who, it is argued, was sent by God only to save white men.

In the last few years a number of scholars in very different fields have turned their attention to the phenomena of messianic and millenary religions. Such religions seem to have appeared throughout recorded history, and by no means only in those parts of the world which are thought to be the special province of the anthropologist. Both Nazism and Communism have been interpreted as secular forms of millenary cult—movements based on a dogma which promises the solution of all problems once the Enemy is removed. In different countries and in different ages the Enemy has been differently pictured. In medieval Europe it was sometimes the priests who were believed to be growing fat at the expense of the poor; also, it was often the Jews. Dr Mühlmann,[1] who has surveyed the ethnographic accounts of such movements in all five continents as well as the records of heretical Christian sects, finds their common characteristic in the resentment of an under-privileged class against those in authority over them, felt particularly if those in authority are regarded as aliens; this situation, characteristic of colonial rule, has its parallels in the early history of Europe.

1. W. E. Mühlmann, *Chiliasmus und Nativismus*, 1961

Some Marxist writers, following the same theme, have seen in them a sort of 'natural' communism comparable to the 'natural' religion that Christian theologians find among peoples who have not heard the Gospel. Dr Norman Cohn,[1] who started by tracing the anti-semitism of Hitler's Germany back to its sources, found that millenary cults in Europe arose among people who were cut off from social ties with any one local group and found themselves in a condition of insecurity; he observed that many of them found their support among the weavers who travelled from one town to another.

The advantage of looking at the millenary movements that have recently given concern to colonial rulers in the context of past European history is that it leads us to reject interpretations based on a supposed special quality of 'primitiveness' in the mentality of non-European peoples. It also shows the inadequacy of the type of explanation in terms of 'culture contact', which, in its crudest form, merely asserts that it is upsetting for peoples of simple technology to be brought into close relationship with peoples of complex technology. Of course it is, but why, and how, and at what specific points? These are the questions that this book seeks to answer, but the answers given in earlier chapters have little bearing on the phenomena of millenary cults. A gloss on the simple 'culture contact' explanation is the theory that the assimilation of Christian doctrine is an intellectual exercise too difficult for some 'primitive minds'. As a result, this theory runs, not only have they misunderstood it and reproduced it in a garbled form, but it has actually led to mental derangement in the prophets of the new cults, and in those of their adherents who during their ceremonies go into trances and show other signs of psychological abnormality. This explanation is offered in ignorance of the fact that most small-scale societies, and some others, believe that the signs of 'possession' are a guarantee of true communication with spiritual beings, and that the dances which are part of their ritual are often intended to induce this state. Cognate, and sometimes combined with, this theory is the view that the rejection of traditional religion has left a void

1. *The Pursuit of the Millennium,* 1957

which has not been effectively filled by Christian belief and practice; the parable of the 'seven other devils worse than the first' might be quoted here, though I do not know that it has been. But there is in fact no void, for although the acceptance of Christianity may result in the abandonment of public rituals, it leaves largely untouched the beliefs and practices through which private individuals seek solutions for their private problems.

It is significant that none of these millenary movements is concerned solely with the 'adoption' or 'rejection' of cultural items, imported objects or the modes of behaviour affected by the bringers of these objects. As the French sociologist Balandier was the first to point out, all are concerned with the relationship of dominance and subjection. There are different ways of envisaging the escape from subjection, and ideas about this may be expressed in different attitudes towards imported objects and towards foreign behaviour. One can divide the millenary movements on the basis of these differences into those that look back and those that look forward.

Of the millenary cults that have appeared during the last century among non-Western peoples subject to alien rule, those that look back are in the minority. The backward-looking cult best known to anthropologists is the one called the Ghost Dance that flourished in the 1880's among a number of tribes of North American Indians. This was a period of crisis in the lives of these tribes. In the space of a few years the buffalo, on which they lived, had been exterminated. They were no longer allowed to range freely, but confined to reservations in which they were expected to settle down as cultivators. Some had bad luck with the land allotted to them, others with the weather, and they were reduced to living on rations issued by the American government.

There appeared a prophet with a message that the Great Spirit of their own religion was angry with them for abandoning their ancient ways, and in particular for insulting the earth by digging it. It was he who had destroyed the buffalo as a punishment. But if the people would follow the prophet's instructions there would be a great cataclysm—an earthquake or a mighty wind—after which the golden age of the past would be restored, the dead would return and be reunited with their living friends, the buffalo would be plentiful and the pale-faces would be destroyed, as would everyone who did not adopt the new cult. The central ritual of the cult was a dance with prescribed steps, which had to be kept up for several nights on end. At the conclusion of such a dance the ancestors would appear; hence the title 'Ghost Dance'. The prophet also adjured his followers to keep the peace among themselves and to refrain from acts that lead to quarrels—drinking, adultery, using 'medicines' to harm others. He offered 'medicines' that would make his followers invulnerable to bullets. These two last features—the magic of invulnerability and the elimination of quarrelling—are characteristic of very many cults of this type. The Christian conception of Christ, as both the Saviour and the bringer of the last judgment to be followed by an unending state of perfection, was not absent from the vision of the Ghost Dance. Sometimes the name of Christ was linked with the approaching cataclysm. But it is significant that here, as in Africa, it is the name, not of a saviour from sin, but of a redeemer from captivity.

The Cargo Cults
The cults of the Pacific area are forward-looking, in the sense that a central feature of their millennium is the possession of all the goods characteristic of the white man's standard of living. For this reason they are usually called 'cargo' cults— 'cargo' being the pidgin-English term used by these island peoples for all trade goods. Many of the cargo cults have sought to attain their end by the destruction of objects associated with the local religion, and sometimes even of all locally made objects. Although they have appeared from time to time ever since there have been Europeans there to record them, they were particularly prevalent at the end of the second world war, and in the years which followed it. Anthropologists who worked in New Guinea at that time have shown how the people's response to Christian teaching, and their disillusionment with it, is what might be expected from their pre-existing ideas of

religion. This is a region where success in any enterprise is held to depend on knowledge of the names of the spirits to be invoked. The magicians are those who know the most powerful names. In such a context of ideas it was easy to see the Christian missionaries as men who knew the name of the spirit that gave the white men their power. When converts have destroyed their cult objects in obedience to mission instructions, they have not been renouncing error, still less repenting sin, but formally transferring their allegiance from the less powerful to the more powerful spirit. Then they have found that the performance of the white man's ritual did not in fact bring them the white man's power. On the contrary, they had lost their earlier autonomy and were obliged to pay taxes and work for foreign employers.

In these circumstances of disillusionment a myth became current that all the trade goods that white men could be seen enjoying were in fact intended for the natives. They had been made by the ancestors in the world of the dead for the benefit of their descendants, but had somehow been diverted by white men to their own use. To every prophet of a cargo cult it had been revealed that the ancestors were about to return, bringing a load of cargo with them that would enable their descendants to live without working for all time. Their return would bring about a reversal of the political order, in which all posts of authority would pass to the natives. Sometimes this process was expected to include a fight for power, but not always. Believers were instructed to prepare for the great day in different ways: often by the destruction of cult objects, in one case by the repudiation of money (and hence of dealings with traders), sometimes by dancing, sometimes by preparing an airstrip or landing stage for the plane or ship with the miraculous cargo, usually by refraining from everyday work and often by killing the pigs on which they depend for meat. Cult members often imitated European ways; by rebuilding village houses in neat lines like a camp, by drilling with dummy guns, by handling pencils and paper or communicating with the ancestors by 'telephone' or 'wireless'. Some leaders organised their own police and bade their followers refuse to obey government orders. The dogma of some cults has included the belief that the missionaries removed from the version of the Bible given to their converts the page which contains the real secret of power. The destruction of ritual objects has often been required by missionaries of their converts. In these cults they seem to figure as the obstacle that stands in the way of the coming of the millennium, and perhaps their destruction may be held to symbolise a transfer of allegiance to the new powers, though not necessarily in the sense of a moral repentance or recognition of 'heathen practices' as evil. One close parallel to the cargo cults has been reported from Africa. This is the Mvungi (pastor, a word used only by Protestants) movement which appeared in 1940 among the Yaka of the lower Congo. This movement had no other content than the command to destroy all objects used in ritual and the promise that thereafter the ancestors would return bringing all kinds of riches with them. It seems to have been as ephemeral as the New Guinea cults.

African Messiahs

But the introduction of Christian teaching to Africa has been accompanied by the founding of a great many breakaway churches under African leadership, not all of them expecting the millennium, and these have maintained their existence over long periods—although they may be subject to fission in their turn. Of millenary movements the most fully documented are those which arose on both sides of the lower Congo in the period between the wars, and are associated with the names of Simon Kimbangu and André Matswa. Simon Kimbangu, who came from a village near Leopoldville and had been a Protestant catechist, appeared originally as a prophet with healing powers; his father had had a reputation for the same gifts. Within a few months from the time when he first became known, in 1921, people were flocking to him in such numbers that the railway company had to put extra coaches on trains running near his village. Like the cargo prophets he required the destruction of 'fetishes', a word which is used in West Africa to describe any object believed to have magical powers, whether beneficent or harmful. Kimbangu had been taught that all were equally evil, and he treated them as such, but he was largely concerned with the elimination of harmful magic, which he, like most people in small-scale societies, saw as the root cause of trouble and dissension among people who ought to live in amity. In his original teaching this by itself was expected to bring about a state of universal peace and happiness. Kimbangu upheld the moral principles of the Christian missions by forbidding polygamy and also the dancing which is judged to be obscene by many Europeans. The Protestant missions, indeed, regarded him as an ally.

Originally called a prophet, Kimbangu soon began to claim the title 'saviour'. He changed the name of his village to Jerusalem, and appointed his own twelve apostles. They and their emissaries conducted their own baptisms, which were interpreted at least in part as symbolic renunciations of sorcery or witchcraft. It was said that a person's sincerity was shown by the way the water ran off him; if his repentance was not genuine his whole face would not be wet when he came up out of the river.

Kimbangu now began to bid his followers defy government orders and refuse to work for Europeans; he believed that this would force the Belgians to leave the country, and that as soon as they had done so the ancestors would return. The faithful were bidden to clear away the weeds from their graves and make paths along which the ancestors could come to the village. Those who did not obey were held to be *ipso facto* sorcerers.

The point had been reached, as it has in most such movements throughout history, when constituted authority had to assert itself; a Catholic missionary who was in the neighbourhood considered that it had waited far too long.[1] Kimbangu was arrested—and almost immediately escaped, thus (for the moment) proving himself invulnerable. His followers began to look forward to the imminent millennium. But three months later he was arrested again and this time condemned to death. The sentence was commuted to life imprisonment. He was

1. R. P. van Wing, '*Le Kibanguisme vu par un témoin,*' *Zaïre*, Vol. XII, 1958, pp. 563–618

taken to Elisabethville, at the farthest part of the Congo, and
spent there the remaining thirty years of his life. The movement
appeared to have been crushed, and the authorities regarded it
as a mere flash in the pan, at most an affair of sectarian rivalry
without political implications.

But their action was exactly what was needed to confirm the
picture of Kimbangu as the saviour. Now there were parallels to be drawn between his story and that of Christ. He had
suffered his own form of martyrdom (though not death) and
would be restored to his followers by God and bring with him
the millennium and the end of European domination. When
Christmas came round distinctions were drawn between the
rejoicing of the white men and the mourning of the Africans
whose saviour was still in captivity. Kimbangists, who until
then had been thought of as allies of the Protestant missions,
now broke with them completely and saw all Europeans as their
enemies.

The French sociologist Georges Balandier has remarked that
the mere fact of Kimbangu's absence made it possible for his
followers to idealise him, as they could not so easily have done
if he had been moving about among them and sometimes dis-
appointing them.[1] Certainly his name was kept alive, not least
by letters home from his banished followers, and he was presented as the saviour in the movements inspired by later
prophets. His fame spread among the Kongo peoples on both
sides of the river. Those on the French side had a prophet of
their own whom they coupled with him, but they could not
ignore him.

The story of the messianic belief which grew up in Brazza-
ville is an interesting one. Its hero, André Matswa, had no
intention of founding a religion. What he did was to organise
from Paris a mutual aid association which was welcomed by the
authorities as an example of African initiative. It had the
additional aim of pressing for the removal of discrimination
against Africans, but it flourished for three years (1926–9)
before protests against their inferior status began to take the
form of passive resistance and it was suppressed. Matswa had to

1. *Sociologie Actuelle de l'Afrique Noire*, 1955, p. 430

be brought from Paris for trial, and this was the first time most of his followers had seen him. Like Kimbangu he spent the rest of his life, for him only twelve more years, in prison and restricted residence. He had brought no message from God nor sought to be regarded as a saviour; a few years later he would have been a nationalist politician. But he became the symbol of African aspirations and the promise of African triumph. He was later believed to have been closely associated with the victories of General de Gaulle, though he died in fact before these had been won. It will be remembered that French Equatorial Africa was the first territory to declare for the General. There is a certain irony in the reflection that a little earlier the approaching war had been envisaged as a German intervention to give Matswa his rights and install him as king, as, on the other side of the river, the defeat of Belgium was hailed as a step nearer the millennium and the kingdom of Kimbangu.

But this is to anticipate. After the arrest and detention of Kimbangu and Matswa, who, it must be remembered, were entirely independent of each other and were pursuing quite different aims, there was a period of quiescence without public manifestations. The next significant event seems to have been the arrival in the region in 1936 of a mission of the Salvation Army. Almost at once the rumour spread that Kimbangu had returned in the guise of a white man and was teaching and healing the sick as an officer of the new mission. In fact it was not Kimbangu, nor a white man, but one Simon Pierre Mpadi, who a few years later founded an all-African church, the *Mission des Noirs*. At first Mpadi found in Salvationist teaching what he said neither the traditional religion nor any other mission could give, 'deliverance from harmful magic, peace within the community and eternal salvation'. To this he added one of the characteristic millenarian prescriptions—the promise could not be realised unless everyone joined the Salvation Army; those who refused thereby proclaimed themselves as enemies of society and sorcerers or witches.

This doctrine had enough in common with that of Kimbangu for many of the latter's adherents to attach themselves to

Mpadi, and a few years later he repudiated association with any Europeans and launched the *Mission des Noirs*, organised on Salvation Army lines with a khaki uniform and a clear chain of command running right down to village level, and with its own scriptures. Drawn in part from the Old Testament, these state unequivocally that Kimbangu is the saviour sent directly from God to the Africans; missionary interpretations of God's will are mere deception. 'We have prayed to God and he has sent us a saviour for the black race, Simon Kimbangu. He is the king and saviour of all black men with the same right [*au même titre*] as the saviours of other races, Moses, Jesus Christ, Mahomet and the Buddha.' 'God did not ask us to hear his word without giving us proof. He gave us Simon Kimbangu, who is for us what Moses is to Jews, Christ to white men [*étrangers*], Mahomet to Arabs.'

In 1955 a report circulated that an 'American Governor General' was about to reinstate Kimbangu. In 1956 the wind of change touched the Kimbangists and also public opinion in Belgium. After petitioning the United Nations to remove the Belgian government and set up one under Kimbangu, they changed their line and represented themselves as a Christian sect with no political aims, which was being persecuted at the instance of the Catholics. Shortly after this they received official recognition under the name of 'Church of Jesus Christ on earth and the prophet Simon Kimbangu'. In 1962 a Kimbangist church was dedicated in Leopoldville with a ceremony attended by members of the diplomatic corps.

A Belgian student[1] who spent nine months in close contact with the present Kimbangist leaders and attended ceremonies at 'Jerusalem' came to the conclusion that the movement was now strictly confined to the religious sphere, and inspired by Christian principles, with the one exception that it had its own local prophet. His informants repudiated Mpadi's religion and also any concern with the detection and elimination of sorcerers or witches. Other recent visitors to Leopoldville have described the Kimbangist church as the religious aspect of the

1. P. Raymaekers, 'L'Eglise de Jésus Christ sur la terre par le prophéte Simon Kimbangu', *Zaïre*, 1959

Abako—the political party of the Kongo peoples, which has sometimes sought reunion with Kongo in Portuguese and former French territory. Yet some Kongo believe that Kimbangu has been reincarnated in M. Kasavubu; and a person claiming to be Kimbangu instigated riots in Matadi in 1959.

Now that Belgian rule in the Congo has come to an end, the Kongo may no longer need to believe in a saviour who has been sent to free them from bondage. Certainly their material problems are no nearer solution. Is it possible that new messianic or millenarian cults will arise to meet new dissatisfactions, or is it more likely that they and others in their situation will turn to secular panaceas?

Some writers, among them myself, have been inclined to suggest a simple correlation between the appearance of these cults and the absence of political representation. It is certainly true that they have been more conspicuous among populations which had no constitutional means of making their wishes felt. But Balandier points out that there are other reasons why aspirations for political change take the form of the expectation of divine intervention. One is that these cults draw support, as the secular nationalist movements do, largely from people who are not equipped to understand the processes of politics and government. The political leaders who have brought their countries to independence communicate with the mass of their followers by simple emotive slogans; the one word 'freedom' is almost enough. But where freedom does not seem immediately attainable and a movement has more limited and specific aims, such as those of Matswa's *Amicalistes* or the village betterment schemes of Yali in New Guinea, some explanation of its purposes, and the action called for, is necessary. This is the problem that faces, and often baffles, community development workers all over the world. The process of rational conviction is immensely slow; the short cut is to endow the desired reforms with magical efficacy. This is not to suggest that the exponents of millenary cults are the charlatans playing on the credulity of simple people that colonial officials have often called them. Balandier's point is something far more fundamental: that there is no means of communication in other than religious terms. Matswa's *Amicaliste* movement appealed in its own terms to the educated minority to which he belonged himself; the unsophisticated mass knew only that Matswa promised *something* to the African, and could interpret the promise only in millenary terms. Matswa himself had no message from God and no intention of becoming the messiah of the Kongo.

Other Independent African Churches

Discussion of messianic movements does not exhaust the subject of independent religions in Africa. Many, perhaps the majority, do not look to a cataclysmic reversal of political and racial relationships. They have come into being for different reasons: the desire for independence of political control, the desire for a separate church for a distinct tribal unit, the desire to retain features of traditional life which official Christianity forbids, and the need for magico-religious treatment of sickness and defence against witchcraft.

The proliferation of independent churches in South Africa has attracted particular attention, and it is possible that it is in fact more conspicuous there than in other countries where nobody has looked for them. Their development has run a different course from that of their counterparts farther north, for the reason that the history of South Africa has run a different course. Where European rule is at an end or is clearly nearing its end, the promise of release from captivity need no longer be the theme of African prophets. In South Africa it is a long time since they ceased to offer this promise. The political protests and aspirations of Africans, which were the concern of earlier independent churches, are now expressed through purely secular organisations, and the African churches accept the situation imposed by white South Africans, and turn *apartheid* into their justification. In the early years of this century African churches preached 'Africa for the Africans', at the time of the Zulu rebellion of 1906 they were promising a reversal of the roles of white and black; but not today.

Today there are two types of church, to which Dr Bengt Sundkler[1] has given the names 'Ethiopian' and 'Zionist'. The

1. B. Sundkler, *Bantu Prophets in South Africa*, 2nd edition, 1961

adherents of the Ethiopian churches aspire to imitate the way of life of the European, and their leaders model their role on that of a traditional chief, while Zionists are more concerned with the revival of traditional modes of healing, and their leaders have the characteristics associated with prophets. The small number of independent churches which have obtained recognition from the government are of the 'Ethiopian' type. In neither class, then, are there protest movements such as have been described in the Congo.

The Ethiopian churches have seen in the acceptance of *apartheid* a way of winning governmental approval at the same time as managing their own affairs independently of any European authority, as is impossible in the mission churches. According to Dr Sundkler they attract the new African commercial classes, and their own leaders are often shrewd businessmen. These are men who do not feel, as wage earners are apt to do, that their case is hopeless under the present régime, and who believe that Africans can better advance themselves in dissociation from Europeans than by seeking their help (as mission adherents do).

But these churches have their own form of conservatism, expressed in the modelling of the leader's role on that traditionally ascribed to the chief, and sometimes in the limitation of membership, at any rate in practice, to particular tribes. Dr Sundkler considers that such churches have often been founded by men whose aspirations for leadership were frustrated in mission churches where positions of authority were reserved for white men.

To maintain his position a leader must show chief-like qualities—courage, diplomacy, wisdom and counsel, and also willingness to listen to counsellors. He is expected to be able to judge cases, that fundamental attribute of an African ruler, and he is approached with the marks of formal respect that used to be given to chiefs. A church leader regards his congregation as in some sense his patrimony, and expects to be succeeded by his son. This last point is characteristic of Ethiopian and Zionist churches alike.

Just as Kimbangu's church provides in fact, if not in form,

a religion for the Kongo people, it is common for Ethiopian churches in South Africa to draw their members predominantly from one tribe. For example, one of the earliest secessions from the Methodist Mission, which called itself the Tembu Church, divided after its founder had declared on his deathbed that he wished to be succeeded by a man from the Gaika tribe. Most of the Tembu members refused to accept this 'alien' leadership.

In the rural areas of South Africa leadership, as distinct from formal authority, appears to be passing from the chiefs, who now hold their position only in so far as they effectively carry out the instructions of the Native Affairs Department, to the heads of independent churches. This is true of Zionist as of Ethiopian churches. Writing of one of the most popular Zionist churches, that of the 'Black Christ' Isaiah Shembe, now under the control of his son, Dr Sundkler says: 'The significant trend is not so much the trek of the prophets to the royal kraal, but rather the pilgrimage of the chiefs to the prophet's temple.'

Another reason for the founding of independent churches is the unwillingness of Africans to accept the condemnation by missionaries of customs which they themselves find worthy of respect, particularly in the field of marriage and sex. No student of social institutions would interpret the difference between African and Christian rules in this field in terms of greater or less self-indulgence, but the Christian prohibition of all sex relations outside of monogamous marriage has commonly been presented in just these terms, and to the missionary eye the taking of a second wife has seemed to be just as much a 'yielding to temptation' as a casual act of fornication would be. It is easy to point out that the founders of independent religions have often been mission teachers who were suspended or otherwise disciplined for sexual offences, but it does not by any means follow that the adherents of these churches join them because they permit sexual licence. Their attitude is rather a refusal to surrender values which are so important to them that they cannot believe that God condemns them, and at the same time an assertion that customs that are despised by Europeans are in fact worthy of respect. With the assertion of the 'African personality' in newly independent states one may expect to see the development of more Christian sects which are willing to accommodate African institutions.

The Zionist churches meet a need which is far more fundamental and far more universal than the political aspirations of a particular epoch—the need for a defence against misfortunes the cause of which is not understood and may in fact be uncontrollable, in particular sickness. Christian teaching here has not destroyed anything; it has simply failed to substitute for generally held beliefs the much more difficult interpretation of misfortunes as occurring by God's will and to be accepted with faith and resignation. The Zionist religions do not 'fill a gap'; what they do is to harness the belief in an omnipotent God and in Christ's miracles of healing to ideas about the magical treatment of sickness which have never lost their force.

Magicians and 'Witch-finders'

Closely similar to them are the 'witch-finding' movements which appear from time to time in other parts of Africa, but seem to be more ephemeral. Many commentators have explained their proliferation as a response to the new uncertainties that the Western impact has created; a few question this, and remark that we do not know what may have happened before governments made it their business to suppress what they regard as fraud, and before anthropologists began to take an interest in witchcraft and sorcery. People sometimes note the emergence of new cults and disregard the disappearance of older ones. These movements do share with the millenary cults the promise of a once-for-all solution—not in their case of political injustice but of the problem of evil conceived in terms of the malicious acts of unknown persons. Those which have moved through Northern Rhodesia and Nyasaland offer as means of detecting sorcery devices learnt from European culture—for example, mixtures in bottles with the combined properties of cleansing repentant witches and sorcerers, destroying those who revert to their evil ways and protecting the innocent.

The belief that success in an enterprise can be ensured by the prescriptions of magical specialists is also as vigorous as ever. People seek new kinds of success, but one cannot often say whether specialists have adopted new techniques or whether their number is increasing. Some thirty years ago a letter was received by the British post office addressed simply to 'Professor Gilbert Murray, D.Litt.' It reached its destination, and was found to come from West Africa and contain a request for 'some powerful learning pills in English and Mathematics'. It has been observed in Ghana that taxi-drivers seek magical aid to get fares and lorry drivers seek magical protection from accidents. And now that people can lose their jobs for being habitually drunk they ascribe their drunkenness to the malice of witches. To my mind these are instances of social continuity in the presence of new cultural factors rather than of social change.

This demand for security in uncontrollable circumstances may be met without the creation of new churches. Prestige often attaches to people who give advice while supposedly possessed by spirits. The activities of such persons have been observed in detail in countries as far apart as Ghana[1] and Singapore.[2] Both observers regard the cults that they describe as an efflorescence, in response to new circumstances, of a form of recourse to spirits that had previously been practised, but had had less importance in the whole complex of magico-religious institutions. In Singapore they can be seen as that part of Chinese religion which could be most easily kept alive in the changed circumstances of Singapore.

One change from what was characteristic of rural China is that religious rites no longer bring together a permanent, defined group of people. The Singapore Chinese have not ceased to revere their ancestors, but the ancestor cult no longer unites a lineage of several generations; such lineages do not exist in Singapore. The head of every family conducts, at a shrine in his own house, rites of worship of his immediate ancestors. As generations pass, those who have become more remote may be commemorated by setting up tablets in public shrines, which may be the property of any of the different

1. M. J. Field, *Search for Security*, 1960
2. A. J. A. Elliott, *Chinese Spirit Medium Cults*, 1956

associations formed by Chinese immigrants in Singapore, and have no exclusive connection with any descent group. In the same way the temples dedicated to particular gods no longer bring together the population of one locality. People worship the god of their association or simply the god of their individual choice.

The associations pay for the upkeep and furnishings of the temples which they maintain, but many of the temples in Singapore are set up by individuals who purport to be actuated by public spirit, but may actually do well out of the thank-offerings of worshippers if their temple becomes popular.

Particularly numerous among these privately promoted temples are those dedicated to spirits who give advice to their worshippers through the mouths of mediums speaking in trance. In 1951 there were estimated to be between 100 and 150 of these temples, at which spirits were believed to give their worshippers advice of all kinds, and charmed objects of general efficacy were sold. As in all societies where there is little medical knowledge, the mediums were consulted most often in cases of sickness, but all kinds of difficulties would be brought to them —family dissensions, the fear of being convicted on a criminal charge, or even bad luck, for the Chinese believe in impersonal unmotivated luck as well as in the activities of evil spirits and resentful ghosts. The medium—or any diviner—must be able to interpret horoscopes, and tell people when their luck will change and what are propitious days for them to embark on enterprises.

The cult of spirit mediums was flourishing in the cities of China in the nineteenth century, and neither the procedures of the Singapore cults nor the explanations and remedies for misfortune that they offer are foreign to well-established Chinese ideas. Their prevalence in Singapore has been explained partly by the fact that this was already the most popular form of approach to ultra-human powers among the section of Chinese society from which most emigrants came, and partly by the fact that the uncertainties and vicissitudes of their new life in Singapore were such as to make them feel even more strongly the need for recourse to occult aid.

Dr Margaret Field, a psychiatrist who spent two years observing the consultation of spirit mediums in Ashanti, came independently to the conclusion that their shrines were proliferating in the cocoa-growing part of Ghana in response to the economic uncertainties that this new but precarious source of wealth had brought with it. Just as in Singapore, the beliefs about spirits who possess human beings and speak through their mouths are part of the traditional religion, just as in Singapore, the shrines flourish while other aspects of traditional religion are, in Dr Field's term, moribund; just as in Singapore, new shrines are the creation of private enterprise. The explanation can hardly be identical, since we are not here concerned with a section of Ashanti society detached from the rest, but must rather be found in the decline of the rituals for which chiefs were responsible, as Christianity has become the religion of literate people.

The Ashanti shrines appear to be usually managed by the kinsmen of the medium. In Ashanti, as in Singapore, it is believed that a man may be chosen by a spirit as its mouthpiece, and that this is demonstrated by his becoming 'possessed'. This does not automatically give him the power of speaking on the spirit's behalf, which requires a period of training by an established practitioner. In Ashanti the first step is for such a practitioner to identify the spirit that has possessed the new medium. He is supposed to discover the name of the spirit responsible—not usually supposed to be one which already has a medium—and to bring down from the sky objects associated with it, to be housed in its shrine. Large sums of money have to be paid for the performance of this rite, and this may be described as the initial capital in the promotion of the new cult. But the new medium and his family may have great difficulty in raising the money, and even though it may be that a successful shrine would repay their outlay, it would be a distortion of the truth to suggest that in Ashanti the promotion of a new cult is just a profitable way of investing money. Both here and in Singapore genuine religious belief, the desire to render service to one's fellows, and the pursuit of material gain are distributed among the people concerned in the organisation of a temple or shrine, and doubtless mingled in the motives of some of them. Different observers may be more impressed by different aspects. Mr Elliott sees the Singapore cults as examples of the commercial exploitation of credulity. Dr Field compares the Ashanti shrines with Lourdes, and the comparison is a just one.

Dr Field recorded for over 2,500 people their reasons for visiting the shrines near which she lived in Ashanti. Nearly 500 of these came to thank the spirit for benefits received, including (nineteen times) the death of an enemy. The largest single category of people seeking help were those who complained of bad luck or, as they put it, 'not prospering'. Some brought their wives or children to be placed under the spirit's protection, some sought protection from specified dangers. Some needed money for some urgent reason; a small number had children who did badly at school, or refused to go. Many complained of sickness of various kinds, of impotency, barrenness, miscarriages, the death of many children.

Of the twenty-nine shrines which Dr Field visited, fifteen were less than ten years old and six were set up during the two years of her stay. Those who are sceptical about the increase in numbers in modern conditions would say we do not know how many went out of business in the same period. But even if we were to reject what is surely a common-sense view, that more people want to consult mediums when they have more to worry about, we might still say that they are bound to flourish when they are all that is left to meet the need that everyone feels, for something to rely on in the face of difficulties that are too much for his own resources.

It is not really a question of much significance whether the number of people who consult practitioners of magic, or the number who believe that they are victims of witchcraft or sorcery, has increased as the range of experience of members of small-scale societies has been extended, and with it the number of possible sources of anxiety. New shrines may indeed come into being to meet an increased demand, new religions to offer an issue out of afflictions that older ones did not envisage. But what has happened is not, or only to a very small extent, to be interpreted as the destruction of one religious system which another has failed effectively to replace. In Africa the acceptance of Christianity has led to the abandonment of much public ritual, and in some places the myths associated with this have also been forgotten. But the indispensable beliefs that account for sickness and misfortune in a way that offers a recourse against them have simply continued to exist, and the indispensable purveyors of this recourse have continued also. What has happened in Singapore is closely parallel, though there it is not Christian teaching that has led to the desuetude of the less 'magical' aspects of Chinese religion.

The attempts of colonial administrations to treat the activities of diviners as fraudulent have done nothing to shake the confidence of their clients in their powers, though they have occasionally succeeded in suppressing particular cults; one of the witch-finding movements that had some success in Northern Rhodesia between the wars died out when its instigator was prosecuted.

Colonial administrators have also tried to deal with the belief in witchcraft by refusing to allow native courts to punish people for something which they can clearly not have done. It is not easy to see what else could have been done by men for whom it is the basis of all justice that the innocent should not be punished. But it is a policy that has never been understood, and if it is the fact that movements purporting to get rid of witches have flourished under colonial rule as they did not before, the feeling that people have been deprived of their recognised means of defence must have contributed to this.

But it is a mistake to think of beliefs in witchcraft as 'just a superstition' which should 'die out with the spread of education'. No doubt the notion of witches as a special kind of being, given to obscene practices and able to overcome the limitations of matter, will come to be less widely held. But the kind of explanation that is expressed in witchcraft beliefs seems to be one that few human beings can do without. Witchcraft beliefs, as part of an explanatory system in which misfortunes are closely associated with moral transgressions, have had their day in those countries where scientific interpretations of the physical world are generally accepted. But explanations of un-desired circumstances which place moral blame for them on the shoulders of imagined enemies, and so by implication relieve people from responsibility for finding solutions for their own problems, are likely to last as long as human beings do. The Communist agitator without whom no subject peoples would be discontented; the colonialists and neo-colonialists who are deliberately keeping their subjects and former subjects poor; the critics who find fault with actors or artists 'out of jealousy'; the examiners who fail candidates for their political views or their racial origins; these are the modern witches.

CHAPTER 7

SOCIAL ANTHROPOLOGY AND
TECHNOLOGICAL CHANGE

*Explanations for reactions to Western technology: psycho-
logical—Cultural—Acculturation studies—In terms of learning theory—Sociological—Malinowski and Functionalism—
Studies of social relationships—Theories which 'cannot
account for change'—A discontinuous technical history—The
theories of Durkheim and Weber—Discussions of the process
of change—Should we seek to establish laws?*

THIS ANALYSIS of the effects on small-scale societies of their
introduction to the world of Western technology has asked the
kind of questions that a social anthropologist asks, and has
answered them from the kind of data that social anthropologists
collect. The questions are rather different from those commonly asked by laymen when they contemplate the changing
societies of the 'underdeveloped' world; they are also different
from those that some anthropologists have asked.

Psychological Explanations
Laymen usually seek explanations of behaviour in terms of
individual psychology. One can readily understand why. In
our everyday dealings with our friends and relations, who share
our values and standards of conduct, we are concerned with
their individual characteristics—what kind of thing is liable to
irritate X and what line of persuasion to take if you want the
co-operation of Y. People with inquiring minds wonder how
cross old Z got that way and how it comes about that M is
such a sweet girl when her parents are so disagreeable; and
there is now a great mass of literature to tell them. A branch of
this literature purports to explain social values in the same
terms as individual behaviour, and this kind of explanation is

readily accepted by the general public because, although it is much more sophisticated than the popular kind, it is on the same lines.

When we are dealing with members of our own nation and our own social class, we take for granted that they are all different and react to similar situations in different ways. It is easy to do this because we are not looking outside the range of people who make the same general assumptions about the right way to behave. As soon as we go outside this field we find ourselves in situations where our assumptions are not shared, and our natural reaction is to think there is something wrong with people who judge their situation quite differently from ourselves; and this 'something' is commonly conceived as a quality of character, or a defect of intelligence. The more closely we are interested in the outcome of such situations, the readier we are with adverse judgments of the other parties to them. Thus, if trade unions campaign for a shorter week, the middle classes inveigh against the laziness of the workers, and if African mothers do not send their children to hospital, missionaries and doctors may say they are too stupid to understand the health instructions they have been given, or even that they are too selfish to consider their children's welfare.

This kind of argument can be generalised into theories that explain all social usages in terms of 'national character'; the sort of assumption made is that numbers of people spontaneously throw their glasses over their shoulders when they drink certain toasts, or refrain from eating meat, because there is some quality of character in each one of them that makes them do so. While it is a popular belief that such qualities are inherited, there is also an anthropological theory that they are implanted by the treatment of infants, which, it is true, varies from one nation to another.

The standpoint from which this book has been written, however, is that the training of infants in the first years of their life is not enough to account for all aspects of their behaviour as adults, and that it does not begin to account for the rules of behaviour by which they find themselves constrained as they grow through childhood into the adult world.

If we are studying social change we have to be concerned with the nature of these rules: why they are kept and why they are broken. All social anthropologists are not equally interested in the kind of change that is going on in the contemporary world; there are many other legitimate subjects of inquiry. But all are interested in the nature of society; that is our study.

Here, however, we come to one of the major divisions among anthropologists: the division between people who think what they are studying is *culture* and those who think it is *social structure*.

Cultural Explanations

The tradition that takes culture for the subject of our study is an old and respectable one. It stems from Tylor, an Englishman whose travels in Mexico inspired work that made him 'the father of British anthropology' and earned him a comparable reputation in the United States. He introduced his two volumes on *Primitive Culture* with a definition of culture as 'that complex whole which includes knowledge, belief, art, morals, custom and any other capabilities and habits acquired by man as a member of society'; a definition which sees man as a social being, moulded by life in contact with other men, but does not mention any significance that might attach to specific social relationships. He continued that this was 'a subject apt for the study of laws of human thought and action'. The complex whole that Tylor described is what later anthropologists have summed up in the phrase 'learned behaviour', and to this day a large number of anthropologists see this as the subject of their study. This has led many of them to conceive of anthropology as a subject related more closely to psychology (the study of the workings of the mind) than to sociology (the study of the working of society). An interest focused on learned behaviour led to an interest in the nature of the learning process, and various theories of social change discuss it in terms of the learning process; it has also led to an interest in those psychological studies which are concerned with the contribution of infantile experiences to the adult personality. It is from these latter that spring the classification of cultures as 'competitive' or 'co-operative', and the attempts to explain these characteristics by the treatment of infants.

Tylor, however, did not limit his definition of culture to thought and behaviour; he added artefacts to the inventory, and thereby condemned his followers to find themselves treating as a single category types of phenomena which no stretch of logic can make into one. His definition was already broad enough to cover the techniques of tool making. By adding to it the objects made, he condemned whole generations of anthropologists to add lists of pots and baskets to their lists of marriage customs, and indeed there was a period when the pots and baskets were in the forefront of the picture. All the heterogeneous items in these inventories came to be known as culture traits.

The controversies of the nineteenth century raged around what were in essence theories of social change. They were not concerned, however, with contemporary, observable change, but with the question, applied to different societies, 'How did it get this way?' This was the problem that Tylor propounded in *Primitive Culture*. He proposed to 'dissect civilisation into details', and the categories which he offered were weapons, textile arts, myths, and rites-and-ceremonies. Under each head, it was suggested, a line of development could be traced; and, except for the heading 'myths', it is certainly true that this could be done for any society of which there were adequate records. Tylor, however, like his contemporaries, thought it should be done for the whole world. It will be noticed that some of his headings concern techniques, and one at least—'rites-and-ceremonies'—refers to social activities; and later he examined the evidence for certain conjectures about the development of the relationships between married couples and their affines. He never suggested that there was any difference between the development of techniques and that of institutions, and so he could not suppose that there need be any difference in the manner of studying them. But there is a major difference; techniques are consciously devised, tried out, improved, whereas changes in institutions very seldom take place in this way. In my belief it is largely the inclusion of 'material culture' in the inventory that has led to the view that was prevalent for so long of culture as a collection of 'traits'. Of course 'material culture' cannot be equated with 'items of behaviour'; it *is not* behaviour and there is no more to say. But the fact that its content can be itemised seems to have influenced the study of 'morals, custom', etc.

The nineteenth-century interest in origins and stages of development drew an immense impetus from the success of Darwin in tracing the evolutionary descent of man. As early as 1860 Herbert Spencer had worked out an analogy between the evolution of societies and that of organisms. He drew ingenious parallels at every point, but committed himself to very little detail about the historical process he was describing; on the other hand, he did not go outside recorded history. More ingenious writers postulated whole series of stages in the undiscoverable past, imagining that they were emulating the biologists who could reconstruct a whole animal from a single bone.

The theory that all human societies must have passed through the same sequence of stages was inspired by the recognition of stages in biological evolution and was supported by the argument of the 'psychic unity of mankind'—an argument which relied not on the biological characteristics, with their psychological correlates, that are common to all mankind, but on the observation that the same kind of ideas, particularly religious ideas, were current in many different parts of the world. It was opposed by the school which maintained that the faculty of invention, which must be postulated to account for advances from one stage to another, is by no means equally shared among mankind; therefore, the complex of 'traits' that we call 'civilisation' must have grown up at certain points where people were particularly inventive, and spread from there by a process of 'diffusion'.

In a sense the diffusionists and the evolutionists conducted their whole argument at cross-purposes. Techniques *are* invented, and whereas one may suppose that the most elementary could have been invented many times in different places, it is equally reasonable to suppose that further elaborations were learnt by some peoples from their neighbours. We can document this process for historical times. But social institutions are *not* invented; we cannot guess how they first came into being, but by looking closely at them as they are we can see something of the subtle interaction of social pressure and individual choice by which they are both maintained and changed. In fact the writers who were most concerned with the evolution of institutions did not postulate the invention of new ones to explain the advance from one of the stages that they assumed to the next; they argued that some section of society was dissatisfied with the *status quo* and insisted on change. Thus men were supposed by Morgan to have rebelled against 'matriarchy', women by McLennan to have found sexual promiscuity offensive to their religious sense.

If the diffusionists had confined themselves to the spread of techniques and the evolutionists to the development of social institutions, one might have regarded the division between them as the prototype of today's division between the students of culture and of social structure. Instead both schools purported to treat techniques and institutions together, though the evolutionists did concentrate their interest on institutions.

The nineteenth-century evolutionary theories, based as they were almost entirely on conjecture, and on the assumption that the culture of the Anglo-Saxon middle class represented the culmination of a process of continuous improvement, came to be discredited as anthropologists learnt to recognise the need to base generalisations on evidence and to avoid easy assumptions about the superiority of their own values.

This left the field largely in the possession of scholars concerned with the analysis of cultures into their component traits, which were sometimes conceived as having no more than an accidental relationship. Culture was described as a 'mosaic', a 'patchwork' or even a 'rag bag'. A critic of this approach wrote (in order to reject it) of the notion of 'items of culture mechanically pitchforked like bundles of hay'.

Acculturation Studies

This is still the approach of a large number of students of contemporary change in small-scale societies, and a whole technical vocabulary, built around the word 'culture', has been developed for their use. Of course such students are not seeking to trace out the sources of the newest elements that have been introduced to the small-scale societies. We know where they come from. But the questions that they are asking are different from those asked by students of social structure.

'Acculturation' studies have sought to establish generalisations of two kinds. One type of generalisation is concerned with the relative propensity of different cultures, or different aspects of culture, to change under the influence of 'culture contact'; the other type with the relative ease with which small-scale societies accommodate themselves to the demands now made on them by large-scale societies.

In the vocabulary which describes these processes, 'cultural traits' are said to be 'borrowed'—a word that perhaps has its origin in the linguist's metaphor of the 'loan-word'—or rejected, or they may be 're-worked' by the borrowing culture. Although it has seemed important to some writers to insist that the influence of cultures in contact was reciprocal, it has usually proved difficult to make this the central theme of any study. When it has been admitted that European art-styles and even sometimes fashions have been affected by influences from outside Europe, that housewives who live abroad often pick up a recipe or two, that in most big cities there are restaurants offering exotic meals, and that less sophisticated Europeans sometimes give credence to magical beliefs of which the Christian church would not approve, the list of 'cultural borrowings' by the West is pretty well complete. The diffusion of Western techniques, on the other hand, is a deliberate process, which was backed at the outset by irresistible force and now is ardently desired by the 'under-developed' world. The 'bearers of Western culture' who went to live among non-Westerners did all they could to establish a replica of their own home life on foreign soil and to maintain contact with the mass of their compatriots at home, and these latter were culturally affected hardly at all by the people to whom their employers sold bicycles and over whom their governments exercised authority. The effects on Western societies of conducting world-wide trade and ruling empires can simply not be understood in terms of the reciprocal influence of cultures. Linton once illustrated the enrichment of a culture by diffusion by enumerating all the objects from different ends of the earth which a normal American might handle or use in the course of a normal day. But he could hardly have maintained that it was the influence of foreign cultures on that of America that brought all these objects within his reach. When Plamenatz writes 'It is not the Europeans who are adopting Asian and African methods and ideas; it is the other way about,'[1] he makes a juster estimate of the balance of modern cultural diffusion.

The process of adoption of alien cultural traits has been considered to constitute a special field of theory and a technical description, 'acculturation'. Acculturation was officially defined by Linton, Redfield and Herskovits in 1936 as comprehending 'those phenomena which result when groups of individuals having different cultures come into continuous first-hand contact, with subsequent changes in the original cultural patterns of either or both groups'. It is a narrower term than 'culture-change', which would include internally generated change, and wider than 'assimilation', which may be 'a phase of acculturation,'[2]

Students of acculturation ask such questions as whether new traits, or elements, or cultural aspects, are more readily adopted if they resemble something already present in the receiving culture (i.e. if they do not entail any radical change in behaviour). According to Herskovits, the leading American exponent of theories of acculturation, such elements or aspects may be 'techniques, attitudes, concepts or points of view'.[3] Linton wrote of a North American tribe: 'The individualistic patterns of the native culture made it easy for certain Indians to take on

1. *On Alien Rule and Self-Government*, 1960, p. 15
2. In a book published in 1938, which has as its sub-title 'A Study of Culture Contact', Herskovits remarked that the term 'culture-contact', which at that time was the key-word in Britain, had been dropped by Americans
3. *Acculturation*, 1938, p. 14

White habits without waiting for the rest of their group to assume them.'[1] And Parsons said that 'new traits tend to be welcomed or readily borrowed if they do not clash with pre-existent traits, or again if they have something in common with pre-existent traits to take the edge off their unfamiliarity.'[2] This phrase implies the conception of 'selective borrowing'. Malinowski, with Africa in mind, justly remarked that we should pay more attention to 'selective giving'.

The exhaustive scheme for the study of acculturation offered by Linton, Redfield and Herskovits as a guide to research all over the world did take into account such variables as the political dominance of one of the groups in contact, and even the reactions which may be produced by 'oppression'; these were confined in the scheme to 'contra-acculturative movements' such as the Ghost Dance, which are in fact remarkably rare. But the whole scheme was built round the notion of 'elements of culture'. Are they forced on people or 'received voluntarily'? How are traits selected? In what order? How are they imposed? Are there some which cannot be imposed? What are the reasons for resistance to the 'traits presented'? And the reasons for selecting particular traits? These include economic and social advantage, further changes entailed by initial changes, and 'congruity of existing culture-patterns'. The 'integration' of traits that have been 'accepted' was treated as a separate problem. The student was asked to look for the conflicts produced by 'the acceptance of new traits at variance with pre-existing ones', for the 'modification and reinterpretation of traits taken over' and the 'displacement of older traits in a pattern' by new ones, and for the personality types of those who 'accept or reject new traits'; also for the influence of particular individuals on the acceptance or rejection of traits.

An irreverent reader who has not found this scheme of study useful cannot help conjuring up pictures of salesmen meeting with sales resistance, of cultural traits spread out on a counter as housewives go shopping, or, in the metaphor suggested by

1. *Acculturation in Seven American Indian Tribes*, 1940, p. 37
2. E. C. Parsons, 'Mitla, Town of the Souls', *University of Chicago Publications in Anthropology*, 1936, p. 521

the word 'mosaic', of some kind of puzzle from which pieces are taken here and there and others substituted.

The conception of culture as a ragbag is appropriate enough for studies concentrated on the sources of different items. But a later phase of the study of culture has sought to find in it some kind of coherence or, as it has been more commonly called 'pattern'. Whereas this word is sometimes used to indicate any kind of regularity, Ruth Benedict meant by it some underlying characteristic or characteristics that could be identified in many different aspects of a culture: she is best remembered for her division of cultures into Apollonian (or, roughly, classical) and Dionysian (or, roughly, romantic). Such differences should be explicable in terms of the personality typical of the 'bearers' of the culture; growing up into a particular type of culture moulds personalities who will be disposed to accept and seek to perpetuate its values. Hence study was directed to the treatment of infants in different societies, and this was correlated with the presence or absence of aggression or competitiveness, not only in individual adults of these societies but in the type of behaviour that was generally approved by them.

Explanations in Terms of Learning Theory

A theory of this type makes it necessary to postulate some new factor to account for changes in approved norms. Such changes are commonly thought of as the adoption by individuals of 'new ways', and explained in terms of learning theory. Thus Barnett in his book, *Innovation*,[1] discusses all the circumstances that may favour or discourage innovation in any kind of society. He reminds us that innovation of one kind or another is going on all the time, and for him no innovation, be it only a new way of making a gesture, is too small to be included in his generalisations. He is concerned with innovations that are imitated and so become standardised as accepted forms of behaviour, but though he recognises that innovations are encouraged in some fields and discouraged in others he does not treat this as a significant fact for the study of social change. Thus he remarks that in

1. H. G. Barnett, *Innovation*, 1953

American cultures changes in technology are expected but not changes in religion, in political structure, or in family organisation; in other words, mechanical inventions are encouraged but social nonconformity is not. This statement in fact puts in a nutshell what seems to some of us the crucial problem of social change among the peoples discussed in this book. For them, it is true, there is no need to make mechanical inventions, but the problem of adjusting themselves to the use of such inventions arises precisely out of the resistance to change that is built into any society, and makes it possible for its members to know what behaviour is expected of themselves and to be expected of others. Barnett might question this statement, since he quotes the Samoans as a society in which everyone is expected to be different from everyone else, not only in inventing songs and dance steps and designs to stamp on tapa cloth, but in 'religion and political organisation'. Nevertheless, the Samoans recognise rules of rank and precedence, and indeed they employ specialist officials to recite the order of precedence among the aristocrats of each district; and they care enough about these rules to have secured a special position for the aristocrats in the constitution given them by the United States. No social order would be possible without some generally accepted picture of the roles appropriate to the relationships in which people find themselves, and some confidence that these roles would be appropriately performed. This confidence is everywhere maintained by constant social pressures tending to reward conformity and penalise deviation. What is interesting in the study of social change is precisely the question what kind of counter-pressure makes nonconformity worthwhile, and this is indeed an aspect of the subject that has practical significance; if it were better understood, the tasks of those who are seeking to improve standards of living by offering technical advice might be no easier, but their nature would be more clearly envisaged.

More recent, more detailed studies by Doob are concerned directly with the type of change discussed in this book. Doob asks what are the most favourable circumstances for the learning of 'new ways' and what happens to the personality of people who 'change' by adopting new ways;[1] and he seeks to find in communications theory reasons why people 'respond more favourably' to some cultural innovations—in this case, assumed to be presented from outside—than to others.

Sociological Explanations

The idea that a student of society should be concerned not with items of behaviour, but with the systematic complexes of rules that organise social relationships, came into anthropology from sociology, and specifically as a result of the influence of Emile Durkheim on the two leading British anthropologists of the twentieth century, Malinowski and Radcliffe-Brown. Durkheim insisted on the importance of 'social facts', which were not reducible to expressions of individual personality nor explicable in psychological terms. Society, he said, was a phenomenon *sui generis*. A society had its own structure, a continuing relationship of functioning parts, interacting to maintain it in being as do the different organs of a living body. 'Collective representations', generally accepted norms of behaviour, arose because in the absence of such norms society could not maintain itself. Of course these can only be located in the consciousness of individuals, but what is more important to the student of society is that every individual grows up into an environment where they are taken for granted, and that in choosing any given course of action he is responding to social pressures and expectations, not simply expressing his personality.

Radcliffe-Brown built all his theoretical work on the concept of structure, but he was not much interested in social change. Malinowski was intensely interested in social change, and approached it through the concept of culture. Nevertheless, his idea of culture was very different from what I have been describing, for two reasons: the theory for which he claimed the name of 'functionalism', and the theory that the 'isolates' into which culture should be analysed were not traits but institutions. He defined an institution sometimes as an organised

1. L. Doob, *Becoming More Civilized*, 1960; *Communications in Africa*, 1962

system of activities and sometimes as a group of persons organised to pursue particular activities.

Malinowski and Functionalism

Functionalism as Malinowski understood it was a challenge to 'conjectural history', the reconstruction of supposed earlier stages of society by explaining existing customs, thought to be anomalous or otherwise inexplicable, as 'survivals' of these earlier stages. Every custom, he maintains, has a function for the people who practise it. If it had not, it would not 'survive' but go out of use, and it is the business of the anthropologist to see how life is carried on in the society that is under his eyes, not to spin theories about what it may have been long ago. This injunction, coupled with the standards of detailed investigation first set by Malinowski, has made twentieth-century social anthropology what it is. Malinowski meant by the function of a custom the contribution which it makes to the survival of the society, or its members, or both; and from this it was an easy step to argue that every society at the moment when an anthropologist examines it is in the condition in which it ought to be, that no change in it could be desired by its own members, and that change introduced from outside could only be for the worse.

Such an attitude logically leads to the view that the diffusion of Western techniques is altogether to be deplored, and indeed Malinowski maintained this position as long as his 'image' of a simple society was drawn from the Trobriand Islands. But after he had visited southern Africa he realised that it had no bearing on the problems of policy in a region where the process had gone much further and could not possibly be halted. He then became interested in 'culture contact', as he himself always called it, not as a phenomenon to be observed with detachment but as a problem to be solved; anthropology, he claimed, could show the way to 'successful culture contact'.

As soon as he became interested in this question he had to find some compromise between his outright rejection of the relevance of history and the study of what is essentially a historical process. He now admitted that the past was significant 'as it lives in the present'—that is in so far as existing institutions derive their value from people's beliefs about their origins. He also opened the door to a certain amount of historical study of colonial policy by his insistence on treating the aims and motives of colonial rulers as part of the process of change. By 'successful culture contact' Malinowski meant recognition of the 'long-term identity of interest' between Europeans and Africans in Africa, perhaps a similar ideal to what was later and equally vaguely described as 'partnership'. In so far as he worked this out in detail, he said pretty much what liberal students of African affairs, anthropologists or not, were saying at the time, and he certainly did not mean by 'successful culture contact' or 'applied anthropology' the removal of difficulties from the paths of colonial rulers. He set his face, as have his successors, against the backward-looking dissection of cultures into their component traits and assignment of these to their different sources; characteristically he argued, not that this was unfruitful but that it was impossible, and from this built up a theory of his own, that the contact of two cultures produced something different from either of the cultures that went to its making, which could not be understood by dissecting it into pre-existing elements.

His conception of the institution as the entity to be isolated for study, which in itself was an immense advance on the idea of a multitude of heterogeneous culture traits all having equal significance, formed the basis of his theory of culture contact. He held that different institutions should be considered separately, as he would have expected them to be in any ethnographic monograph, but that the data should be fitted into a tabular scheme of a kind which he liked to use when teaching. He thought these 'charts', as reminders to the ethnographer of the data that he must obtain, were as essential a part of his equipment as note-book or camera, and I believe that some of his most eminent pupils have found them so. As a teaching device for stimulating thought about relations between social phenomena which were not immediately obvious, the 'blackboard chart' was superb; as a system of categories for the presentation of results it was less valuable.

Nevertheless, Malinowski regarded his 'three-column approach' as his essential contribution to the study of culture contact. He required the observer, dealing with any particular institution, to place in opposite columns the corresponding or contrasted characteristics of the institution concerned in 'African' and 'White' culture, and between them what resulted from the contact. In a volume published after his death,[1] he offered schemes to cover witchcraft, warfare, diet, chiefship, land rights and 'segregation policy'. The last could hardly be called an institution, and its presence in the list is the key to the difference between Malinowski's theory and his practical approach. His 'White' column was not in fact a list of the European counterparts to features in his 'African' column. It was even headed 'White influences, interests and intentions'; in other words it described the ideas held by the dominant group about the institutions of the subject majority and their attempts to change these. He was concerned in fact with the ways in which men pursue their interests when these interests bring them into contact with societies whose institutions differ from their own. The real ground of his difference from the acculturation school could be put as the recognition that cultures do not have 'interests or intentions'. One of his favourite aphorisms, 'It is sometimes valuable to state the obvious', was illustrated when Fortes enunciated the epoch-making truism that 'Individuals and communities react under contact; and not customs'.[2]

Studies of Social Relationships
This phrase comes from a set of essays by pupils of Malinowski which were based on their experiences in the study of culture change—as we still always called it then—as Fellows of the International African Institute. Fortes' contribution, though still couched in terms of 'Culture contact', anticipates the change of emphasis that has led most of us to think of society

1. *The Dynamics of Culture Change*, 1945
2. 'Culture Contact as a Dynamic Process' in *Methods of Study of Culture Contact in Africa*, International African Institute Memorandum XV, 1938, p. 62

or social relations as the central theme of our study, and to hold that this change is more than a verbal fashion. 'Culture contact,' he wrote, 'is a process of the same order as other processes of social interaction, both in the literate societies of Europe, America and Asia and in the pre-literate societies of other parts of the world,' and 'the anthropologist must work with communities rather than customs. His unit of observation must be ... a unit of common participation in the everyday political, economic and social life.' With the second of these statements Malinowski would of course have agreed; it is his conception of the co-operative group with a common purpose that makes the bridge between Tylor's view of culture as a sort of outfit of possessions, material and mental, and the view of structure as it was defined by Radcliffe-Brown as a network of relationships between persons, or, as Linton would have put it, a system of statuses each with its appropriate role. To study social structure in this way implies looking for permanent groups linked by continuing common interests and for permanent relationships of superiority or subordination, co-operation, competition or hostility; it implies a different map of society, with more positions plotted, than the Malinowskian analysis into institutions; but the co-operative activities that Malinowski called institutions have a large place in the picture.

Now to recognise the importance of social structure, and to give it priority as a problem for investigation, is neither to deny the importance of culture nor to use another word for the same thing; it is to ask a number of highly significant questions which many students of culture do not ask. I have tried to build this book round answers to that kind of question. Social relationships are made manifest through cultural behaviour, and this is what the inquirer sees first; it is his key to the analysis of the structure which he learns to perceive as he observes the regularities in people's behaviour and in their comments on behaviour. Society and culture, Nadel said, are two facets of the same reality. Yes, but they are not *the same thing*; it is quite possible to make extensive inventories of cultural facts while largely disregarding social relationships, and many writers have done so.

Theories which 'cannot account for change'

Do we need *a theory* of social change? If we say that we do, we imply that it is normal for societies to remain unchanged for generations, and that a special explanation is called for if they do not do so. My contention is that both continuity and change result from the inter-play of the same social factors. However, some theories of society have been criticized specifically because they 'cannot account for change', and these call for some mention. Such theories are exaggerated versions of the generalisations about the processes by which respect for social norms is maintained, without which the study of society could not have advanced very far. The criticism applies particularly to those which use the concepts of 'function' and 'equilibrium'. Durkheim's use of 'function' has been mentioned in passing. The word actually came into sociology with Herbert Spencer, for whom it implied an analogy with the relation between the parts of a living organism and the contribution of each to its survival. Thus, heart, lungs or digestive tract, each has a function within the human body; if any fails to perform its function adequately we are sick; if any ceases to perform it at all, we die. The word was taken over by Durkheim, who is better known than Spencer to most British anthropologists. Durkheim, when indicating how he would use the term, expressly drew the analogy with the organism: 'the function of respiration is to introduce into the animal's tissues the gases that he needs to keep alive', he wrote.[1] He went on to say that asking what is the function of the division of labour amounts to looking for the need to which its corresponds, and that 'function' was the only correct word to use. The division of labour was not created deliberately to achieve some end, and it would be wrong to speak of its 'aim' or 'purpose'.

Malinowski developed the use of the term very much further. He opposed the theories current when he began teaching, which explained aspects of the customs of primitive society as 'survivals' from previous forms of organisation. His insistence on the study of such societies as 'functioning wholes', in which nothing was meaningless, resulted in the development of new

1. *De la Division du Travail Social*, 1926, p. 11

208

standards in fieldwork, and did in fact lead to most fruitful analyses of supposedly meaningless customs. But he passed from the argument that everything in society was meaningful to the argument that everything was indispensable; and the *reductio ad absurdum* of this argument is that every society at the time when someone happens to record its customs is in the only state in which it could possibly be and can never have been in any other.

But before he had developed the theory of the correspondence of institutions and needs to such an extreme point, he did emphasise, and rightly, the view that the small-scale societies have managed to produce institutions adapted to the kind of life that their environment imposes upon them, and that the inadequacy of these should not be simply assumed by people who take other institutions for granted without reflection. This respect for the institutions of others is, in my view, the most important contribution that the popularisation of anthropology could make in the field of public opinion. Of course to treat alien institutions with respect is not, as some have pretended, equivalent to insisting that they must be maintained in being for the aesthetic satisfaction of anthropologists.

However, the analogy with an organism does lead to further analogies with states of sickness and health, which cannot be developed very far without leading logically to the conclusion that a society is unhealthy if it is not maintaining itself in the condition in which somebody thinks it ought to be at the moment when it is under observation. Durkheim thought society was in a healthy state when it was cohesive, and when it reacted vigorously against breaches of its rules; and it is clear that social change does involve the breach of rules. Yet to Durkheim the very function of the division of labour is to create new relationships of interdependence, which link people over wider areas, and to weaken the cohesion of small units based on kinship or neighbourhood.

What Durkheim saw, and what everyone must see in a society subject to rapid change, was that there are fields of behaviour where norms are fluid, and situations where people are subject to incompatible expectations and strong pressures from

H   209

different directions. This is uncomfortable for them, and they may find that they cannot perform adequately all the roles in which they find themselves cast, and this again may be hard on some of the people whose expectations are disappointed. Anthropologists, with their eyes fixed on the small-scale societies experiencing dramatic change, have not always recognised that such discomforts are felt in any society: this bias is being corrected as we extend the field of our interests. But it is fair to say of the British attitude that our feeling that the difficulties of the small-scale societies are especially great sprang in part from that sense of responsibility for them which is the reputable aspect of paternalism.

In my judgment the metaphor of equilibrium leads to greater difficulties, and this although some of those who use it apply it to changing situations. Thus Radcliffe-Brown wrote that social structure was 'a condition of equilibrium that only persists by being continually renewed like the chemico-psychological homostasis [sic] of a living organism'. When the equilibrium is disturbed 'a social reaction follows which tends to restore it'.[1] But sometimes the disturbance and the reaction lead to a modification of the system, and if the disturbance is serious this may take a long time. We may ask when we know that a society is in equilibrium, and even the most eminent anthropologists give us rather dusty answers.

The word gained vogue among sociologists with the writings of Pareto, but British anthropologists do not quote Pareto, and it is possible that to those of them who use this term it means something less specific than it did to him. Pareto's equilibrium was a mathematical relationship between different social forces, such that a decrease in one must be compensated by an increase in some other, and anthropologists have never applied his analytical scheme to their data. In fact it seems that to those who write about the re-establishment of equilibrium, the word has no more meaning than another that was used by Radcliffe-Brown, euphoria; both mean a condition of social well-being which is judged by the observer to exist, though he asserts that it is in some way felt by the society.

1. Introduction to *African Political Systems*, 1940, p. xxii

The word has also been used to mean some kind of balance of power. It is in this sense that Fortes and Evans-Pritchard have written of the equilibrium of political systems. Thus they state of certain societies which do not recognise a single central authority that 'stability is maintained by an equilibrium at every line of cleavage and every point of divergent interests in the social structure'.[1] These societies are divided into corporate lineages no one of which has in fact sought to dominate the rest. There are records of many such societies, but there are others again in which a single lineage *has* asserted domination over non-members living on its territory, and one might even guess that this is how hereditary monarchy came to be established. Moreover, equilibrium in this sense refers to the distribution of the power to enforce respect for rights, and this is a much narrower meaning than that given to the word by Radcliffe-Brown.

All the concepts in common use that imply that there is value in maintaining an existing social order—balance, harmony, equilibrium, adjustment and various others—have been attacked by Myrdal as excuses for doing nothing in the face of social injustice. It is certainly true that they may be so used. It seems to be also true that people like to feel themselves part of an ordered society, and since most of them are not very imaginative, they tend to see this in terms of what is rather than what might be—particularly so, of course, if they are beneficiaries of the existing order. But if the maintenance of any given social order may perpetuate injustice, it is still true that people cannot live in society without some sort of order, and that this order is maintained by the kind of reaction that Durkheim called the assertion of social solidarity and Radcliffe-Brown the restoration of equilibrium. It is equally true that such reactions, since they are prompted by moral sentiments which are taken for granted and not by the rational assessment of situations, may often penalize changes in behaviour that an observer might—rightly or wrongly—consider desirable.

But it is only if equilibrium is considered as a *natural* condition of society—and then only if the conception of adjustment

1. *African Political Systems*, p. 14

to a new equilibrium is disregarded—that this can be described as a theory which makes it impossible to account for change. One would be more inclined to make this criticism of those theories of 'enculturation' which imply that people are moulded by their cultures into characteristic types of personality, that they attain adulthood having been conditioned to behave in the appropriate way to every situation that confronts them, and that some new process must be postulated to account for their failing to do so.

Any theory of society which recognises that moral norms are not automatically followed is able to account for social change. The fact that there are sanctions for the breach of social rules, and that these are often effective, does not prevent one from recognising that changes come about when they are broken with impunity on a sufficient number of occasions. We may agree with Durkheim that it would be disastrous if all rules simultaneously were broken with impunity, without committing ourselves to the view that all change, because it is disruptive of social order as it is, must be disastrous.

We are indeed frequently reminded, and not least by the work of social anthropologists, that contemporary small-scale societies have certainly not existed unchanged since their first appearance as human beings. All the societies that we know today must in the past have gone through experiences which radically transformed them, and some can recall changes, at any rate in their political structure, in recent times. For the few remaining peoples who are wholly nomadic the crucial event of their history must have been the domestication of animals. The discovery of cultivation, which made it possible to live in permanent villages instead of wandering about looking for wild fruits, must have been another such. We know that some peoples have conquered others and incorporated them into centrally controlled states. It is thought probable that the kingdoms in the south-western part of Uganda were formed through the domination by pastoral invaders of an agricultural population already settled there, but the extent to which an upper class has maintained its pastoral way of life has varied greatly in the different kingdoms. From certain Ganda traditions it has been possible to construct a picture of the kind of see-saw struggle between a king and his retainers that Weber saw as the perennial problem of patrimonial rule. Leach has shown how the Kachins of Highland Burma lived in polities which oscillated continuously between democratic and aristocratic rule.

But, when all this has been said, the most dramatic of these changes happened so long ago that it is impossible to picture them, and they may have happened so slowly as to be not really very dramatic. The political developments resulting from the conquest of one small-scale unit by another are more recent, in some cases recent enough to be remembered in a manner that is closer to factual record than to myth. But even these do not lead the people who have experienced them to see their societies as subject to change.

Fortes, who was one of the first anthropologists to criticise the notion of a social integration so complete as to eliminate conflict, has also described the attitude towards tradition of the Tallensi of northern Ghana, among whom he lived for two years. He shows how, although there is room for both conflict and competition, the Tallensi themselves do not see their social order as something that has changed in the past or should change in the future. Not only do they 'have no history in the sense of a body of authentic records of past events'; they 'think of their social order as continuous and persistent, handed down from generation to generation'. Their mythology 'postulates a beginning for what has existed ever since'. They have no conception of a past 'when people lived and behaved differently from today'.[1] Fortes goes on to say this does not mean that Tale customs never change, and gives examples, all of which are responses to the political control and economic opportunities brought to the Tallensi with European rule.

It is alleged that anthropologists are driven to picture the societies they study as unchanging because there are no records and they themselves do not stay long enough to observe the changes that take place. This is not entirely true, for some anthropologists have traced changes in political systems by using records of such facts as the manner in which chiefs have

1. *The Dynamics of Clanship among the Tallensi*, 1945, pp. 24, 26

succeeded one another. Such changes may have resulted in the imposition of tribute on people who had not paid it before. In some cases we know this to be so, and in others we know that the authoritative settlement of disputes was imposed on, or sought by, people who had previously relied on self-help. But the business of wresting a living from the soil, and the co-operative relationships which this entails, do not appear to have changed significantly over the centuries that preceded the 'scramble for Africa'. Perhaps the introduction of new crops by the Portuguese in the sixteenth century led to some re-organisation of labour forces that we cannot now trace. Since then there is no record of any change in techniques that would call for substantial changes in the organisation of work or the holding of property.

A Discontinuous Technical History
But what is far more significant than the question whether the small-scale societies of Africa, or for that matter the peasant societies of India, changed much or little before the nineteenth century, is the irrefutable fact that the changes which then came to them were stimulated by forces wholly external to them. This discontinuity in the technical history of the 'under-developed countries' contrasts sharply with the experience of those where the tradition of scientific experiment is indigenous and one technical invention has grown out of another. The same could be said, of course, of those areas within Western nations where a peasant economy still prevails; the small number of studies that have been made by social anthropologists in Mediterranean countries have found that they are facing problems of adjustment very similar to those that have been described in this book.

This discontinuity is significant when one is considering the generalisations that have been made about social change, for one consequence of it is that the most illuminating writers have little to say about the characteristic experience of the societies that have been 'developed' from the outside; their propositions do not take the possibility of a discontinuous technical history into account. Such writers as Durkheim and Weber were concerned with the cumulative process that had created the type of society in which they lived. The 'elementary forms', as Durkheim might have called them, were considered, in relation to the analysis of contemporary phenomena, either as a starting-point or as illustrating general principles of social structure which could be found in the most diverse types of society. So the discussion of this particularly dramatic type of social change has been left almost entirely to anthropologists.

It is the contention of this book that, if a thread can be traced throughout the history of human society, it is the thread of technical invention. Successive inventions, as they have increased man's control over nature, have made it possible to link wider circles of people in continuing social relationships to which recognised norms of conduct apply. Some inventions, in weapons and communications, have increased the possible range of governmental control; the most recent have increased the possible range of material comforts, and made it necessary for people who wish to enjoy these comforts to be organised for economic co-operation on a scale undreamt of two centuries ago.

The Theories of Durkheim and Weber
But the writers who have conceived these changes as essentially changes in the nature and extent of social relationships have mainly been concerned with European history, and with a past much more recent than the time when our ancestors knew nothing of the wheel or of writing. They have traced certain irreversible developments in social institutions, but they have begun the story at a later stage. Nevertheless it is to the writings of sociologists that social anthropologists at present must look for the kind of generalisations about social change that answer the kind of questions they are asking. Those whose work has proved most illuminating have been Durkheim and Max Weber. The former was concerned with small-scale societies mainly because he sought to establish universally valid principles and expected to find them there in their simplest form. He was not greatly concerned with processes of development, though in his discussion of the division of labour he contrasted the social

structure of the Iroquois with that of industrialised society with its ever-increasing specialisation of functions, not only economic. He argued that the greater the specialisation in a society, the more it would resemble an organism in which every part had a function and all contributed something to the whole. Such a society would have a solidarity superior to that in which community of feeling rested merely on the likeness of the parts —as he held it did in societies where people were grouped on the basis of kinship, groups which he compared to the rings of the earthworm. The process which he envisaged is essentially that creation of a wider field of social relationships that has been described in this book, but this was not the aspect of it that interested him. Indeed he was more concerned to draw contrasts than to trace developments, and all he had to say about the process of increasing division of labour was that the pressure of population must have made it necessary. Moreover, at the time when he wrote, the ethnographic data available were very inadequate.

Max Weber confined himself to societies of which there is historical record. He was primarily interested in the distinctive characteristics of Western capitalist society and in the prerequisites for their emergence, rather than in the historical process by which it had come into being, and he rejected any theory of clearly defined stages of social development. Yet he could not help observing certain trends which seemed to be continuous in recent history, and which he summed up as an increase in rationality. In religion a rationally argued ethic grew up beside an older reliance on magic, though he did not suggest that purely magical ideas were replaced by purely ethical ones. In economics what he called the 'speculative' pursuit of gain, usually in alliance with political power, came to be supplemented by the rational calculation of relations between outlay and return, involving characteristically the organisation of production as well as of trade. In politics he saw the distinguishing feature of the modern state as the rule of law and administration by an impersonal bureaucracy, chosen for qualifications acquired in a specialist training, employed on contract and not expected to make profit out of their offices, and acting predictably in accordance with recognised rules and with loyalty not to a person but to impersonal standards of good administration.

As the circumstances necessitating the rationalisation of government Weber saw the increasing geographical extension of political units, the creation of standing armies, and, more recently, the public demand that the state should undertake an increasing range of activities. The increasing centralisation of political power proceeded *pari passu* with that of economic power. In a modern state the final holder of power *owns* the means of administration, whereas in earlier historical periods the ruler's subordinates themselves owned these means, and so were in a position to assert autonomy if they wished. Weber enumerated the means of administration as 'money, buildings, war material, vehicles, horses or what not'.[1] He remarks that it is the expansion of the money economy that makes the creation of a 'rationalised' bureaucracy possible, as it makes it necessary. Some of the circumstances that he mentions, such as the problems of the maintenance of standing armies, have no counterpart in the small-scale political units with which this book has been concerned.

Weber did not aim, as Marx did, to identify universal principles that would be found in operation in every society and must determine a parallel course of development in them all. He was concerned with types of institution and their correlates, and his types were abstractions to which actual societies approximated more or less. Many of the latter combined features of different types; ancient Egypt, for example, combined 'patrimonial rule' with bureaucracy. Thus it is in one sense not a relevant question whether his type of 'patrimonial rule'—the rule of the head of a large household—or of 'traditional domination' corresponds to anything observed in small-scale societies. But some of his generalisations about the way things might be expected to happen do imply concrete mental pictures, and some of the pictures are rather unlike those that would come to the mind of a social anthropologist.

1. 'Politics as a vocation', in H. H. Gerth and C. Wright Mills, *From Max Weber*, 1947, p. 81

His discussion of the patriarchal kin-group, in which authority was maintained by the fear of 'magical evils that would befall the innovator and the community that condoned a breach of custom', implies a period when the *patria potestas* was much more effective than anthropological study has usually found it to be. Much recent work on African societies discusses the younger generation's resentment at subordination to the elder, the impatience of young adults for independent control of their share of the patrimony and their efforts to anticipate the distribution which ideally should await the death of the senior man. In India and China too it has been shown that the ideal of family solidarity was no more than an ideal except in particularly appropriate circumstances. Granted that sickness and misfortune were often interpreted as punishments for disrespect towards authority, this did not preclude the possibility of such disrespect.

Weber's references to the sacredness of tradition and the arbitrary power of the traditional ruler, which tradition itself confers upon him, give an impression of greater 'irrationality', in his sense of the word, than really characterised small-scale states. Certainly the claim to hereditary rule is made valid by tradition alone, and the belief in the sacredness of the ruler's person is not a matter of rationally argued ethics; but it is only in ritual matters that he is constrained, or supported, primarily by the sacredness of tradition. In his secular role what is expected of him is formulated in terms of ethical principles, though admittedly these do not form a coherent philosophy, and so far from himself modifying tradition by arbitrary action, he is more likely to meet with various forms of resistance or non-co-operation if he acts in an arbitrary manner. Again, when Weber says[1] that 'every system of domination will change its character when its rulers fail to live up to the standards by which they justify their domination', he overlooks the possibility of which Gluckman has reminded us,[2] that hostility may turn against an individual while his office is held as sacred (or taken for granted as much) as ever. Yet, in describing the

1. As quoted by Bendix, *Max Weber, An Intellectual Portrait*, 1960, p. 300
2. *Custom and Conflict in Africa*, 1955

characteristic forms taken by the struggle for power in societies organised in different ways, Weber has suggested possibilities which anthropologists have found illuminating. He does not suggest that at any given time this struggle can have only one outcome; he is concerned more with the nature of the groups that may be expected to compete.

There is value too in his identification, as one type of polity, of 'traditional domination' which is made legitimate by the mere fact of having supposedly been 'always there', since it reinforces the observation of many anthropologists, that small-scale societies do regard their institutions as unchanging.

Only Redfield[1] has treated the whole historical process as a continuum, in his discussion of the world-view of people living in societies at different levels of technological development. Redfield accepted the definition of civilisation as consisting in the life of cities, and he saw as the first stage of development the pre-civilised, before cities existed. Next he considered 'peasant' or 'folk' societies co-existing with cities and in some respects influenced by them. In the relationship between the city and the folk society he traces that process of destruction of the moral order of the smaller unit, and its later reorganisation as part of something more inclusive, which has been one of the themes of this book. His final stage is that at which men consciously seek to improve their own institutions.

Discussions of the Process of Change
The question how change actually comes about in a small-scale society—a different question from that of the nature of the changes that have been observed—has been discussed by a philosopher, Professor Dorothy Emmet. She has shown how the concept of roles which can be played in more than one way allows for greater flexibility in the interpretation of social processes than the picture of a social system consisting in interdependent institutions which reinforce one another and by their combined action keep the whole system going.[2] In such a picture

1. R. Redfield, *The Primitive World and its Transformations*, 1953
2. 'How far can Structural Studies take account of Individuals?', *Journal of the Royal Anthropological Institute*, 1960, pp. 191–200

every institution has a function, and if it is further argued that every function is indispensable, we are back at the point where every change is pathological. Firth has remarked that the interdependence of institutions in the simpler societies really means just that the same persons will be found to play roles in each institution.[1] It is easy to demonstrate, and it has been demonstrated, that, in a population of many millions, which can be called a system in virtue of having a common government and body of laws, organisations can exist which do not reinforce other institutions or contribute anything indispensable to the maintenance of the whole. But even in small-scale societies there can be conflict between the different roles expected of an individual, and this raises for him questions of moral choice. Such conflicts may be inherent in the institutions of the society, and this is where, Professor Emmet suggests, moral creativeness should lead to social change; yet we do not find recorded instances of such changes in the societies that have been studied by social anthropologists. Professor Emmet finds her earliest examples among the Hebrew prophets. But she does, I think, make the case that societies of simple technology are not so heavily weighed down by inertia that nobody feels dissatisfaction.

Leach has gone further and argued that the structure of small-scale societies contains within itself the possibilities of choice from which social change can arise, and indeed that without some room for manoeuvre they could not continue to exist at all. He instances the case of societies where property is held by unilineal descent groups. Each individual belongs, without the possibility of choice, to one and only one such group, to which he is affiliated through *one* of his parents. But he is free to choose what relationships he will establish among kin linked to him through the other parent, and will choose according to his own conception of his own interests. Earlier he had shown how, among the Kachins of Highland Burma, rival ideas of social relationships, the one aristocratic, the other equalitarian, can be appealed to by the same individuals at different times, according to what best suits their interest at the moment, and

1. *Elements of Social Organization*, 1951, p. 89

how people in a position to rise in society can claim high hereditary status by editing the record of their own descent.[1] 'In all viable systems,' Leach writes, 'there must be an area where the individual is free to make choices so as to manipulate the system to his own advantage.'[2]

The question at what precise point a social structure can be said to have changed has been discussed only by Firth, on the basis of his own studies of the New Zealand Maori,[3] who have experienced immense social changes, and the people of the tiny island of Tikopia, who have experienced relatively few, but whom he was able to visit twice at intervals of a quarter of a century and thus document the observable changes over a generation. Those which could be observed in Tikopia could not all be ascribed directly to external pressures, and indeed they have been far less extensive altogether in remote Tikopia than in the places described in the body of this book. The increase of population, leading to a pressure on the food supply which was dramatically increased by a severe drought and hurricane just before his arrival, was in his view the latest phase in a race between population and resources which must have been going on for at least a century. He observes that such population movements must have been responsible for more social changes than anthropologists allow for. But he also tells us that neither these nor external pressure had significantly changed the institutions of Tikopia society. Their effect had been to alter the balance of power and wealth between different sections of a society organised as it 'always had been', or at any rate was conceived as having always been.

Firth's scheme for the analysis of social change is more detailed than that of any of his predecessors.[4] The changes in the balance of importance in groups the organisation and formal relationships between which remain constant he calls social movement. The re-ordering of status relationships which occurs when a man succeeds to a position of authority, or

1. E. R. Leach, *Political Systems of Highland Burma*, 1954
2. E. R. Leach, 'On Certain Unconsidered Aspects of Double Descent Systems', *Man*, 1962, p. 133
3. *Economics of the New Zealand Maori*, 1959
4. *Social Change in Tikopia*, 1959, pp. 340–6

indeed whenever an heir takes on the social responsibilities of a dead man, he would call social replacement. It is not quite clear where in this scheme would come the creation of new affinal ties by a marriage. The creation of independent lineages by fission he calls social multiplication. I doubt whether these terms are likely to be much used, but their existence is a reminder that no society is completely static.

Then, however, come a number of categories for the description of what have been generally regarded as phenomena of social change. Firth distinguishes between the changes which are primarily organisational and those which are primarily structural. Organisational changes are those in which something that has always been done is done in a different way, structural changes those in which types of social relationship are radically modified or may even disappear. Structural change itself he analyses into changes in the structure of ideals (or the norms of conduct which people will assert to be the right ones) in the structure of expectations, or what people will in fact expect others to do, and in the structure of action, or what they in fact do. These categories are perhaps more likely to be valuable as a guide to field-work—as headings under which information should be sought—than as topics on which one might seek to establish generalisations.

Should We Seek to Establish Laws?
If the study of society is to be regarded as scientific, must it seek to establish laws? And must it succeed in doing so? On this subject anthropologists are at variance, while students of the physical sciences would refuse them the right to claim the status of laws for their generalisations, and laymen are indignant at the idea of law in human affairs.

Much of this controversy arises from the ambiguity of the word law, and from failure to be clear about the kind of field in which laws are sought. Among anthropologists the leading writer to have repudiated the quest for laws is Evans-Pritchard, who in 1951 remarked that anthropologists had never produced anything 'remotely resembling what are called laws in the natural sciences', but added that they should not try to, since social systems are not comparable (as Spencer and Radcliffe-Brown maintained) to physiological systems nor yet to the planetary system. Anthropology, he said, is more like the kind of historical study which deals with institutions and 'it therefore seeks patterns and not laws, demonstrates consistency and not necessary relations between social activities, and interprets rather than explains.' Some of these distinctions may be rather hard to follow, though Evans-Pritchard himself described them as 'conceptual and not merely verbal differences'.[1] More recently he has elaborated his views on the value of such comparative study of institutions as can be made by the reading of history, views with which no contemporary anthropologist, least of all one concerned with social change, would disagree, and which were beginning to be whispered even during Malinowski's lifetime. In this second formulation he refers briefly to the failure of anthropologists who have sought to establish laws, but this time he is concerned less with the consequences of the organic analogy than with the spurious laws of evolution and diffusion propounded in the nineteenth century. He remarks further that in any case we have now given up generalisation for the detailed study of particular cases, so that it would make no practical difference if we stopped talking about laws.

One of the questions implicit in this discussion is whether the social sciences are *as good as* the natural sciences; and a quite different one is whether they try to put human beings on the level of mindless objects, and in particular deny them the capacity for moral choice. On the answer to the first question (assuming that merit resides in the type of generalisation established) anthropologists disagree.

A scientific law states an invariant relationship between factors. It 'predicts' in the sense that if certain quantitative factors are known, others can be quantitatively calculated. It does this in virtue of the scientist's grasp of the principles underlying their relationship. It has been remarked that this understanding is not obtained by counting instances, by generalising from particular cases: 'physicists do not hunt out regularities in phenomena, but investigate the form of regularities whose

1. *Social Anthropology*, 1951, pp. 57–62

223

existence is already recognised.'[1] Physics is an explanatory science, whereas natural history is a descriptive one.

One or two anthropologists believe that in time we shall arrive at generalisations which can be expressed in equations. Most of us are content with something more akin to natural history, and we can certainly claim that we describe the characteristics of society more fully, more accurately, and with a deeper understanding of the factors at work, than the layman whose 'common sense' leads him to generalise—that is to claim to have perceived regularities—on the basis of mere unsupported assumptions.

But some laymen suppose we are claiming to foresee an unchangeable future, forgetting that any generalisation about what is likely to happen merely says 'This is what usually has happened in such a situation'. We have been rebuked for our presumption in even seeking regularities in a volume, dealing with the same sort of subject-matter as this book, which is being widely read. 'Social analysis,' writes the author, 'particularly when dignified with the name of social science, is always tempted to a determinist view of human affairs, since its business is to detect "laws", or at least regularities, in social development. It is constantly necessary to remember that no such iron laws exist—only human choices springing from values and beliefs. There is no intrinsic necessity for African societies to follow our own route of development, or for the family system to disintegrate.'[1]

This allegation is not supported by reference to the findings of any social scientist, and in fact it is no more than a succinct statement of a popular prejudice. If the 'laws' that we seek are no more than 'regularities', they are not 'iron laws' and there is no need to warn the public against the consequences of our yielding to temptation. In fact, as I have been trying to show, the regularities that our analysis has found are not regularities in development at all, but the regularities which at any given time make it possible for the members of a particular society to know what they can expect of their neighbours and their neigh-

1. S. Toulmin, The Philosophy of Science, 1955, p. 44
2. G. Hunter, The New Societies of Tropical Africa, 1962, p. 332

bours of them. It is precisely for concentrating on this kind of regularity that some anthropologists have been accused of disregarding the fact of change. Moreover, this kind of regularity cannot be contrasted with 'human values'. It is the expression of human values.

The specific example of the disintegration of 'the family system' is an interesting illustration of the difference between contemporary British values and those of the nineteenth century —that is if I have understood its by no means clear purport. In the nineteenth century it was assumed that the nuclear family, in which parents have the sole and full responsibility for their own children, was morally superior to the extended family of small-scale societies, particularly since the extended family was often polygamous. Now we have learnt more about the extended family as a source of mutual aid, and can sympathise with individuals who have lost its support. Yet close analysis does suggest that the nuclear family is better able to seize the opportunities open in times of great social mobility, and that, where economic and religious co-operation are found in other forms of association, there is little incentive, as there is little need, to maintain a large body of kin as a co-operative unit.

But perhaps what is intended is the statement that 'the family' is disintegrating in Europe, and the assertion that this is no reason why it should disintegrate in Africa as well. Social analysts of the European scene do not in fact believe that 'the family' is disintegrating, and if anyone has the impression that this is happening in Africa, this is either a pure impression or a conclusion based on reported observations; it is not deduced by any social scientist from any 'law of social development'.

A truer statement of the degree of confidence with which a social scientist estimates what will happen is this by Leach: 'I do not for a moment want to suggest that the future development of any particular Kachin community is in any absolute sense determined or predictable. On the contrary I hold that individuals and groups of individuals are constantly being faced with making choices between several possible correct alternatives. But circumstances may operate in such a way that particular kinds of choice are likely to appear more advantageous than others. This does not mean that the outsider can predict what choice will be made, but only that one may predict what choice is likely to be made given certain assumptions about the value system and rationality of the actors.'[1]

This book has been concerned entirely with human choices springing from values and beliefs. It makes some assumptions about the kind of values that lead people to make the choices they do, assumptions such as every student of society must make, since it is not possible to discuss human behaviour without assuming that it is directed to ends. It also notes certain common characteristics of small-scale societies, 'regularities' if you like, correlated with those limitations of technique which oblige small groups of people to co-operate in every aspect of social life.

Most of the assumptions with which I have written this book would be regarded by my colleagues as truisms. In summary, in any society a certain type of behaviour is held to be appropriate to each of the recurrent social relationships which make up the social system. This means, not that every detail of behaviour is prescribed, but that the limits of what is permissible are generally recognised. Those who cross these limits suffer for it in disapproval, unpopularity or more material punishment; nevertheless people sometimes think it worth while to do so. In every society people regard as good the esteem of their fellows, the possession of material wealth and the ability to influence the actions of others, and they manipulate their social relationships in pursuit of these ends. This kind of activity produces some degree of social mobility even in small-scale societies where change in the total system is very slow. In the recently industrialised societies, new opportunities of attaining wealth and power have been created by the introduction of new productive techniques, and of the new political systems without which these techniques could not have been introduced. I think it would be possible similarly to correlate many changes in European society with the creation of new opportunities, and that this is implicit in the works of many sociologists. A general

1. *Political Systems of Highland Burma*, p. 228

theory of the forces making for social change would have to account for the flourishing of invention at particular periods, but such a theory is not necessary in examining societies which have received modern inventions ready-made. New opportunities can usually be seized only at the cost of some disregard of existing obligations, and where to seize them necessitates a radical change in mode of life there will be friction between those who gain by the change and those who lose by it. If the discomfort which results is to be taken as evidence of a pathological condition of society, this should not lead to the conclusion that all change is for the worse, or that it puts such a strain on small-scale societies that they need to be protected from it. But it is useful for people who are concerned in trying to guide the direction of change, be they nationalist leaders, Peace Corps members or emissaries of the United Nations, to know where the points of friction are, and they can learn this only from the analysis of social relationships.

SUGGESTIONS FOR FURTHER READING

FOR READERS who are interested in pursuing further the study of social change in various fields, the following books may be of interest:

On Changes in Family Life and Kinship Structure

Arthur Phillips (ed) *Survey of African Marriage and Family Life*, Oxford University Press for International African Institute, 1953

P. Marris, *Family and Social Change in an African City*, Routledge & Kegan Paul, 1961.

R. T. Smith, *The Negro Family in British Guiana*, Routledge & Kegan Paul, 1956

R. P. Dore, *City Life in Japan*, Routledge & Kegan Paul, 1958

M. Freedman, *Lineage Organisation in South-eastern China*, University of London Press for London School of Economics, 1958

J. Djamour, *Malay Kinship and Marriage In Singapore*, University of London Press for London School of Economics, 1958

On Changes in Economic Organisation

F. G. Bailey, *Caste and the Economic Frontier*, Manchester University Press, 1957

T. S. Epstein, *Economic Development and Social Change in South India*, Manchester University Press, 1962

Polly Hill, *The Gold Coast Cocoa Farmer*, Oxford University Press, 1956

W. A. Warmington, *A West African Trade Union*, Oxford University Press for Nigerian Institute of Social and Economic Research, 1960

On Urbanisation

UNESCO, *Social Implications of Industrialization and Urbanization in Africa South of the Sahara*, 1956

J. C. Mitchell, *The Kalela Dance*, Rhodes-Livingstone Institute Memorandum 27, 1956

A. L. Epstein, *Politics in an Urban African Community*, Manchester University Press, 1958

P. Mayer, *Townsmen or Tribesmen*, Oxford University Press, 1961

G. W. Skinner, *Chinese Society in Thailand*, Cornell University Press, 1957

On Changes in Political Relations

T. L. Hodgkin, *African Political Parties*, Penguin 1961

G. M. Carter (ed.), *African One-Party States*, Cornell University Press, 1962

J. S. Coleman, *Nigeria*, University of California Press, 1958

On New Religions

B. Sundkler, *Bantu Prophets in South Africa*, 2nd edition, Oxford University Press, 1951.

P. Worsley, *The Trumpet Shall Sound*, Macgibbon and Kee, 1957.

K. S. Burridge, *Mambu*, Methuen, 1960

G. Shepperson and T. T. Price, *Independent African: John Chilembwe*, Edinburgh University Press, 1958

INDEX